THE HIDDEN CHILD
BOOK CLUB REMEMBERS

THE HIDDEN CHILD BOOK CLUB REMEMBERS

An Anthology of Holocaust Stories

*Edited and with a foreword
by Susan Gold*

Full Court Press
Englewood Cliffs, New Jersey

First Edition

Copyright © 2016 by Susan Gold

All rights reserved. No part of this book may be reproduced or transmitted in any form or by any means electronic or mechanical, including by photocopying, by recording, or by any information storage and retrieval system, without the express permission of the author, except where permitted by law.

Published in the United States of America
by Full Court Press, 601 Palisade Avenue
Englewood Cliffs, NJ 07632
fullcourtpressnj.com

ISBN 978-1-938812-73-6
Library of Congress Catalog No. 2016930509

Grateful acknowledgment is made to the *Hidden Child Newsletter* of the Hidden Child Foundation / ADL for permission to reprint Susan Gold's "Memory and History."

Book design by Barry Sheinkopf for Bookshapers.com
(www.bookshapers.com)

Colophon by Liz Sedlack

TO THE MEMORY OF OUR FAMILIES,
*and to all those
who survived the Holocaust*

FOREWORD

In January 1990, half a century after World War II, the Anti-Defamation League in New York City, and a small group of Hidden Children, began an earnest effort to hold an international gathering of some 1,600 "lost children" from twenty-eight countries. From the very beginning, the ADL has taken us under its wing and provided much help in solving logistical issues, such as phones, program arrangements, and media expertise. Most importantly, we received a home and office space in the ADL building in New York.

This project took an enormous amount of work and co-ordination, and we are forever grateful to the organization for their help and support.

Late in 1991, after resolving many challenging and logistical issues, a multitude of us Lost Children from across the world excitedly packed into a New York City hotel to find each other: for comfort, to reconnect with long-lost friends whose Holocaust experiences we shared, and, more importantly, to cry and to find ourselves. The purpose of the gathering would be to share memories, help those who were too young to remember, and, foremost, tell the world that a significant number of people who had lost their childhood during the Holocaust were still with us.

More than a million children were murdered during the Holocaust. The few who survived were hidden in convents, orphanages, haylofts, and sewers. Many had been given away by their parents to Righteous Christians. A few adolescents survived by working in concentration camps.

The Hidden Child Foundation has helped us by holding conferences, meetings, concerts, book readings, film screenings, and get-togethers for our members. All these ongoing programs have been nurturing and sustaining. We always enjoy learning about new subjects and look forward to visiting and schmoozing with one another.

In addition to the gatherings, we have a Hidden Child Book Club, which I facilitated under the ADL umbrella many years ago. We are some fifteen adults, all Hidden Children, survivors from many countries. Our common history and understanding of our lost childhoods, and our love of literature, have brought us together. After many years of reading and discussion, we decided to write our stories, each very personal, and publish this collection.

Most of us were very small children during the war. Since then, we have invested our energies in educating ourselves and rebuilding our lives. Although the Shoah is always with us, many of us were too vulnerable to look back, let alone to write about that time.

It is only after retirement, after building up our families and contributing to society, that we have the time and greater emotional security to cope with the past.

All of us in the Hidden Child Book Club have realized that time is running out. We lived through an unprecedented period, when the whole world turned upside down, when the sun was extinguished, and the sky became empty. Some feel that we chose life and dared to survive and now have an obligation to write about it. Imagine, men and women in their 70s and 80s writing about these extraordinary events etched in our minds so many decades ago! My sincere thanks to them all for the courage to share parts of their journeys. Each story is a world unto itself, and will amaze our readers.

Dr. Gady Levy, Director of the Temple Emanu-El Skirball Center, then generously provided the funding to make this book possible. Rabbi Joshua Davidson was gracious enough to discuss my ideas about the book and our club activities, and welcome us to the Ivan M. Stettenheim Library at Temple Emanu-El.

Barry Sheinkopf, editor and publisher of Full Court Press, helped us through moments of great difficulty. I thank them all.

Temple Emanu-El has been most welcoming in offering the impressive and comfortable Ivan M. Stettenheim Library to the reading club, where we meet monthly to discuss literature about the Holocaust as well as contemporary fiction and nonfiction.

When all is said and done, our stories will remain our legacy for our children and grandchildren—a historical record of which they can be proud. Some of our stories offer a broad view of our cities, villages, camps, and ghettos, and some tell of resistance, escapes, or the rescue of children. Rarely do we portray the Germans with any insight. The Germans are a kind of *deus ex machina*, a mysterious evil force in the realm of humanity, and is hence impossible for us to discuss. The German is nameless, his face seen only from a distance, peering out from beneath his glowing swastika military cap.

In some small way, our stories are a repayment of our debts to the dead. For many of us, a common motif in survivor literature is a sense of guilt. There is no doubt that our families and our peers were more deserving to live than we ourselves. But we now have a sense of satisfaction at having been able to survive that time of murder and carnage. We have created new families with children and grandchildren named after those who were killed.

With the passage of time, there are not many Hidden Children left. The crater left in our hearts for the families we lost will never heal. But our lives reveal the yearning for dignity in our struggle to endure, and the need to maintain our humanity under inhumane circumstances. After all, it is only by luck that we live.

These stories communicate the truth that we were saved largely through chance and twists of fate, and only rarely through personal attributes. A truck rounded up Jews on one side of the market square and not the other. A Nazi officer liked the face of a young girl and chose to sleep with her, and have her clean his boots and press his uniform, rather than shoot her. A man survived a death march because of a flannel jacket thrown to him by a hunter. We, who were worried that our stories would go with us to the grave, can now hope that our anthology will preserve our individual legacies.

Since we retired, after building up our families and contributing to society, we have had more time and greater emotional security to cope with the past. But all of us in the Hidden Child Book Club realize that time is running out. We lived through an unprecedented time. Some of us feel that we chose life and dared to survive and now have an obligation to write about it. Each of us has a survivor story to tell, and each story has its own agenda. The fact that every person has a different saga, and that each memoir is a world unto itself, continues to be a source of amazement for readers and appreciation for our writers.

We hope these stories will be more meaningful to young readers than learning about the Holocaust from history books. Perhaps this collection will also represent a useful addition to the educational curricula in schools that teach the history of the Holocaust.

While most of these stories dwell principally on suffering and devastation, and resonate with a sense of lost childhood, we have rehabilitated ourselves through them and functioned professionally during the day even if terrifying dreams of anguish, despair, and murder creep up on us at night. We hope that the sense of cleansing and renewal will embrace those who read this book as well.

—Susan Gold
January 2016

TABLE OF CONTENTS

Danielle Lerman: *The Eggs*, 1

Susan Gold: *Memory and History*, 5

Felice Zimmern Stokes: *A French Survival*, 15

Clare Ahrens: *Nathan's Story 1941–42*, 31

Toby Levy: *My Story As a Hidden Child during The Holocaust*, 35

Lola Bielski Dzienciolski Kline and Bella Bielski Dzienciolski Rubin: *The Borrowed Child*, 45

Carl Hausman, *My Brother, Günther*, 69

Charles Roman, *My War Years History*, 73

Judith Gertler, *Have U.S. Passport—Will It Save Me?*, 81

Ruth Gruener, *How Acts of Kindness Saved Lives— Mine and My Parents'*, 87

Zahava Szàsz Stessel, *Growing Up In the Holocaust Days*, 91

Rina Nudel, *Dearest Mama*, 101

Helga Shepard, *A Web of Tragedies*, 107

Essie Schor: *Fighting the Nazi War Machine*, 117

THE EGGS
Danielle Lerman

M<small>Y MOTHER AND</small> I <small>LIVED</small> in a tiny French village during the war under the control of French Nazi authorities. Food was rationed and very scarce then. Farmers had a little more to eat, and were able to barter. I was a teenager. One day, on a borrowed bike, I went searching for food among them.

Only one lady farmer agreed to part with six eggs after I told her it was for a *malade* (sick person). I put them in my backpack and, elated, headed back to the village.

I decided to take a short-cut along the railroad track, and rode without incident until I saw a man in a black beret coming from the opposite direction. There was no room for two bikes on the same path. I got off mine to let him pass, but that toothless pig, instead of saying thank you to a kid, extended his arm and gave me a good push. I fell hard on the tracks. I resumed biking, crying bitterly. I knew what had happened to my precious cargo.

When I got "home," my mother started crying with me. She had thought some arrests had been made, or that I had been hurt. When I told her the story, and that the eggs had been broken, she said, "That is all? Don't cry. I'll make a cake." And she did. Where did she get the flour, the sugar? She invented the flourless, sugarless cake.

Soon after the first egg episode Oeuvres de Secours aux Enfants, the OSE, placed me in a poor convent in the city of Limoges. My mother remained alone in the village, under the watchful eyes of the police.

After the miracle landing in Normandy, the nuns allowed me to go and visit her. It was a two-hour train ride.

I did not make it to my destination. The French partisans had blown up part of the tracks to prevent Nazis from fleeing. I was stuck in the middle of a field, but I knew the region.

I started to walk towards the closest village, hoping to find a room at the only inn, but there was nothing available. I continued to the railway station in order to spend the night on a bench.

Then I heard little wooden clogs running after me on the cobblestones; a curly blond young woman offered to take me home with her, which I accepted. Her gray-haired mother gave me her own bed, and during the night the cat came to check on me. I still see them all so clearly in that small flat.

I slept like a baby, and in the morning the mama made me a delicious breakfast of three eggs. I had not had any for so long. This little family with a Christian heart refused any kind of payment.

Soon I was on my way to visit my own mother ... about an hour's walk away.

A few days later, I sent these angels a thank-you letter, but I am not sure if it ever reached them. There was street fighting there: Houses and bridges were partially destroyed. So not all egg stories are about rotten people!

Bio Note

Danielle Lerman was born in a small town in Poland. Soon after, her parents immigrated to France.

The rest of their family remained in Poland or left for America.

During the war, she had a very limited education in France. She was separated from her parents and brother, and survived under the protection of the OSE. She spent some time in children's homes and in a convent. After the war she was reunited with her parents and, eventually, her brother. The family in Poland did not survive.

Lerman's first job in New York was with an airline; then, with great pleasure, she joined an Israeli tourist company. She spent the rest of her working years in tourism and has traveled extensively. She is now retired but has wonderful memories of her many trips and the beautiful lands and people she visited.

MEMORY AND HISTORY

Susan Gold

MUCH HAS BEEN WRITTEN about voluntary and involuntary memory in the study of history, literature, and psychology. Some historians believe that memory and history are different and, sometimes, even contradictory. History can be suspicious of memory and often aims to suppress and destroy it. History is disciplined scholarship involving validated, academic research of archival and archaeological material with the aim of writing an objective, impartial record of a subject or period.

Memory, by contrast, implies subjectivity and partiality—what we "feel" happened rather than what "actually" happened. It is a personal process of engaging with the past, a process that has ethical, psychological, and historical dimensions.

Only historians know the difficulty of this second kind of scholarship, which has, as a result, created still another field of study, that of historiography, the study of history. Historians and historiographers have both pored over many archives to write about The War against the Jews. Many volumes of research and scholarship have produced, and are still producing, huge bibliographies.

For us here, history and memory are *not* separate and contradictory; they are fluid concepts cut from the same cloth. We share ideas and feelings meaningful to the past and its remains. We navigate both rivers—memory and history—simultaneously, and the task of remembering makes all of us our own historians. Each is not only a keeper of a history and memory but has the added responsibility of imparting a legacy—the collective, shared memory of whole communities that are no more. Our families, children and grandchildren, and humanity as a whole join us in articulating that legacy.

But I want to go beyond the metaphor of "history and memory" to understand their significance. I am intrigued by yet another aspect of the subject—the *sites and environments* of memory, the play of memory and history from a very personal point of view. This idea was the driving motivation behind my memoir, *The Eyes Are the Same*.

For child survivors, only remnants of our prewar experiences remain, and the more time passes, the more difficult it becomes to navigate the chaos, carnage, and murder we witnessed during the Holocaust. We keep our pre-war recollections alive in the warmth of our traditions and in the repetition of our ancestral rituals. But the sites and environments of our history have been completely destroyed.

Poland, before the Second World War, was home to nearly 3.5 million Jews, the largest Jewish community in Europe. Jewish identity in Poland and the Ukraine had very deep roots dating back to the fifteenth and sixteenth centuries. With the annihilation of that community, the collective memory of a shared past was wiped off the face of the Earth. Today, our environments of memory exist as tourist curiosities—in Kazimiezh, a Jewish neighborhood in Krakow, in the Krakow Klezmer Festival, and in the other visited sites, the cemeteries and the former death camps.

In the maelstrom of our emotions, we recall only

the presence of the evil we endured and we hate the places of murder. Our ruins are unlike all others. The best example I can give of a monument to our grief is the Janowska site near Lvov. This memorial depicts a woman reading to a child whose head has been cut off.

My childhood was lost, wiped out, in Poland and the Ukraine during the Holocaust. My parents and I survived the war in a bunker under a barn in the small village of Podhirce, in Western Ukraine, during the period called *Judenrein*. I had no idea what *Judenrein* was, nor was I old enough to understand the traumatic events I was living through, but my mother said that the members of our family were being "resettled" and had to go away. I only knew that they disappeared, and that we had to hide from people who wanted to "kill" us.

As a child I had no way of comprehending the concept of death. I could remember but was not old enough to comprehend the traumatic events I was experiencing. I *did* understand that I had to be silent, not move around, and be very still in the bunker. My parents' lives depended on my being a silent, hidden child.

That unnatural siege went on for almost two years, until we were liberated by Russian soldiers on their way to Berlin in the spring of 1944.

There was no joy or victory after liberation. We could not tell anyone who we were or why we were going back to Zloczow, the town where I was born and where my grandparents lived.

We returned to a ravaged and destroyed place, hoping especially to find my grandmother and younger brother who, as a toddler, cried and fussed and therefore could not stay in the bunker with us. Both had been killed.

By 1947, we ended up in Deggendorf, a displaced persons camp in the American Zone of Germany. I was a pre-adolescent girl of eleven, with long, curly hair and wild, frightened eyes.

I was allowed to run around, laugh, cry, and sometimes scream. I could make friends with other children and adults who taught me how to play cards and Ping-Pong. I also learned how to ride a bicycle, and I spent my days learning to balance while pedaling fast, almost streaking, cheeks red, hair flying, around a beautiful lake bordered by graceful weeping willow trees.

Feeling free, I managed to erase, in every way I could and as quickly as possible, the terror and trauma of the Holocaust. Indeed, many of us wanted to hide our Holocaust provenance quickly, willing our past to vanish, slipping into the present.

Regardless of the difficulties associated with that transformation, gone were the terror and fear of sewers, attics, bunkers, orphanages, and concentration camps. The War against the Jews was no more.

My American uncle found us on a list of Holocaust survivors, and he soon brought our small family to America, to New York City's Delancey Street, or *Delançé* Mother would say using her best French pronunciation. I also made friends with American soldiers and truly began to feel "American" when they treated us to Coca-Cola and, most importantly, American bubble gum! Knowing how to blow bubbles, and chew gum for a long time without swallowing, made me a de-facto American ready for *Delançé* Street!

In the U.S., my parents and I were plunged into Williamsburg, Brooklyn, where Mother and Father somehow bought a small grocery store. She, a law student before the war, was a true survivor. She worked six and a half days a week, fourteen hours a day. She kept inventory, talked to the salesmen, helped customers, and lugged cartons and bottles while my father, depressed and disabled, sat sadly at the cash register, studying the newspapers, a dictionary at his side.

Having never attended school, I entered seventh grade and somehow mastered the English language.

Since education was of utmost importance to us, six years later Brandeis University found me and awarded me a full scholarship.

I had no idea what an "out-of-town college" meant but instinctively knew it would be better than life on South Second Street in Brooklyn. I traveled to Brandeis along with friendly strangers who were driving their own daughter to college. I was one of the very few freshmen arriving with another family for that chapter of life.

I willed my past to vanish completely. I found it threatening to speak Polish, impossible to speak Ukrainian. I studied Russian history, language, and literature because it was "safe" from associations with my terror yet had a familiar Slavic base. It was also my father's native language, and the young Russian soldiers who liberated us had been kind and had smiling faces.

In America, I fled into the present and towards visions of a better future, putting thousands of miles between me and what used to be called home, never wanting to see it again. But I was always ambivalent. I willed my past to be a desert, but I could never entirely let go of that terrible territory between my fifth and twelfth year. Surely lost souls are entitled to be remembered!

With time, I slowly allowed my past to resurrect itself. Eventually, an entire ghost city began to live in my head, claiming frozen emotions and causing endless anxiety. Unearthing long-buried recollections that I had never dared to disturb, tapping into my childhood, I began to breathe, dig, move around, and describe what a child, innocent of adult self-knowledge, had experienced and seen.

Memories were as I remembered them when I began writing. Were they true? Is a memoir fiction or nonfiction? Now, more than seventy years after the Shoah, many of us speak of memory, creative work, and our legacy because there is so little left of our past. We also live in a world of instant communication: computers, sound bites, political spin, blurbs, iPads, a lonely disconnect between the virtual and the real world in which anything and everything may rapidly appear and disappear.

I can only say that I was able to work imaginatively, to preserve I think the integrity of my own memoir. That book enabled me to take myself back into the heart and mind of the child that I was, a child who speaks to us from a distant time and place and becomes the guide to the sights and sounds of another, happier time, as well as to the pain and fear we endured.

Other genocides are now in the limelight. Man's inhumanity to man, repercussions of continuing racism and intolerance, march on. No doubt these atrocities are producing their own hordes of child survivors we have yet to hear from.

Bio Note

Susan Gold, a volunteer at the Hidden Child office, is a retired expert in Russian business development. She has also taught at the Columbia University School for International Affairs. Her Holocaust memoir. *The Eyes Are the Same* (Full Court Press). was published in 2007.

A FRENCH SURVIVAL

Felice Zimmern Stokes

I WAS BORN IN WALLDÜRN, GERMANY—a small town in the Black Forest region—on October 18, 1939, about six weeks after Germany invaded Poland.

I pieced together everything in this story after my sister, Béate, and I came to the United States in early February 1951. Before then, I knew nothing about my past. It was as if I had been walking in a fog. Little by little—through people who had brought us over, from others at a Jewish agency in New Jersey who had information about us, from speaking to the townspeople who remembered our parents in our hometown, from reading as much as possible about the period, by writing to the International Tracing Service in Arolsen, Germany, and, finally, from letters my parents and relatives wrote from a concentration camp in France, I found out about additional portions of my life. However, there still are some remaining mysteries.

MY PARENTS, SISTER, I, and the rest of our family (how many I do not know, but I know for a fact about two out of three of my father's brothers who were also living in Walldürn)—and all the rest of the Jews there—were deported in 1940. In the *Macmillan Atlas of the Holocaust*, by Martin Gilbert, I learned that "on October 22, 1940, the German Government deported more than 15,000 German Jews from the Rhineland to an internment camp in France, at the foothills of the Pyrenées." The place where we were taken to was Camp de Gurs. As it turns out, it was only a holding center, or, as Vichy, France, called it, a "shelter camp," which was in reality a concentration camp. Nearly two thousand of the deportees died as a result of the conditions in that camp.

My sister and I were separated from our parents. From the letters we were given, we learned that our mother, Lydia Bloch Zimmern, had a difficult time trying to visit us in the camp. Eventually, as I understand it, in January 1941 a French-Jewish agency called Oeuvres de Secours aux Enfants (OSE, a social welfare agency) was able to take us out of the camp. How this was done, we have never been able to find out. We were taken to a place called La Pouponnière (a nursery that was located in Limoges). When conditions became dangerous, we were hidden elsewhere. Actually, my sister was taken out after she reached her fifth birthday, since no children older than five could live there. I was eventually moved to a small village about two hours from Limoges, near Chateauroux, in the South of France. The small town, called La Caillaudière, was near Vendoeuvres. I have been told by residents of the area that a member of the French underground went through a nearby village, asking if anyone wanted to hide a Jewish child. [A few years later, I found out that it was really a Jewish social worker—who in fact worked for the OSE—who took me and found a new place to hide me.] An old farm couple, who were non-Jews, agreed to take me in. Their names were M. et Mme. Gaston Patoux. It was because of the Patouxes, with the help of the OSE, that I survived. While I was with the Patouxes, they were always on the lookout for the Nazis who might come to take me away. It was very dangerous for the Patouxes as well. I remember Mme. Patoux hid all of her jewelry underneath the ground, and anything of value as well. She never slept in a nightgown, but in her slip, always ready to run if we had to.

When I came to them, I was almost three, and I stayed with them until I was six. I was their little girl. I felt very close to both of them. For me, they were my parents — my "Mémée" and "Pépé" (my nicknames for them). M. Patoux took me many times to the village store. Their son, Roger, took me for bike rides through the countryside.

When the time came, I went to school there. I even went to church every Sunday with them. During the time that I lived with the Patouxes, I was known as Félicie Patoux. I'm sure that quite a few people in that very little village knew that I was Jewish (and how extremely dangerous it was for me to be hidden in their town), but no one said anything to give me away. I didn't even know I was Jewish.

My sister, Béate, was not with me at the time that I lived with the Patouxes. (I didn't know I had a sister either.) She had been hidden, in turn, by a family in Limoges, and then by nuns. We were re-united three years later, in 1945. She stayed with me and the Patoux family for about three months at the end of the war in Europe. Late in 1945, the OSE placed us in a Jewish orphanage called Draveil. The OSE wanted to bring us back into Jewish surroundings. However, being separated from the loving Patoux family was very painful for two small children—especially for me, as I had lived with them for as long as I could remember. We were able to visit the Patouxes for one summer vacation in 1947. But I do not remember that very well. As a matter of fact, I do not remember the two years at Draveil at all. The trauma of having to leave the Patouxes was too much for me.

We were then taken to another orphanage in Taverny (called Chateau de Vaucelles), near Paris. I found out much later that Taverny was the orphanage where Elie Weisel had lived in 1946.

We lived at Taverny from 1948 to 1951. It was quite a pleasant experience. It had a very warm, Jewish, religious atmosphere: Each child had gone through the same trauma as my sister and I. We had wonderful counselors. As a matter of fact, I remained in contact with our former counselor, Hélène Ekayser Weksler, who had suffered in the war, as well, until her death—another very sad loss for me!

In late January 1951, my sister and I were sent to the United States—to New York (so we believed), because we had an aunt and uncle (in Buffalo) who thought we would have a better life in the States. But that was not to be. (Eventually, I found out that the reason we couldn't stay with them was that they didn't have the room in their apartment, since my aunt's mother lived with them, as well as her brother and my aunt and uncle's son. The most unbelievable irony of all was that a very wonderful couple, not related to us, had wanted to adopt us and take us to the United States. But our aunt and uncle had refused!)

When we arrived at the Port of Newark, we were met by three social workers—none of whom spoke French—and since we spoke no English, it was quite hard and painful for us to understand. Since my sister was thirteen years old (two years older than I), she understood a bit more and started to cry, knowing what awaited us. We were taken to a children's home in Newark (run by the Jewish Child Care Association) for about two years before this home was disbanded. My aunt and uncle were not allowed to see us for a few months, because the agency knew how painful that would be for us. (I never forgot that event!)

I eventually went to live with my second foster family, a very good one—Toby and Murray Geller, in Linden, New Jersey, who had two sons, Jack and Michael.

At that point, I was ready to begin high school and attended Linden High School for four years; and that went quite well. I also became very close to the Gellers and their relatives, which was quite important for me. (To this day, we consider ourselves family.)

In the late '60s—when I began to deal with the pain of having lost the Patouxes—I decided to try to contact Mme. Patoux. (M. Patoux had died in 1950.) I found her address and wrote that I wanted to visit her. She wrote back when she finally heard from her "chère petite Félicie," and she shouted it from her open windows. She met me at the train station. She was then about eighty years old and had lost all of her teeth. But we recognized each other immediately when she brought me into the town next to her little village; all of her relatives, and quite a few of the townspeople, remembered me. We were in a circle, and they came up to me, one by one, and kissed me. As you can imagine, we were all in tears! When we were alone, Mme. Patoux gave me all the pictures she had saved when I was a little girl, and she told me stories about the time I lived with her in the '40s. She said, "People from a Jewish agency kept taking you away from me! They always wanted to check up on you and whether we were taking good care of you, because when you first came to us, you were in terrible health and emaciated!"

Sometime later, as an adult, I found out what had happened to my parents. I'd had a feeling that they might have been deported to Auschwitz. However, I'd also fantasized that one day someone could call me and tell me that they were still alive. But that was not to be. In 1972, when I visited my counselor, Hélène, in Paris, she said that perhaps I should look through a book called *Memorial to the Jews Deported from France, 1942-1944*, by Serge Klarsfeld. Hélène said that, if my parents had gone through any camp in France, their names would be listed in this book, which contains those of almost all of the Jewish victims in France, their nationality, age, and birthplace. It represents, as M. Klarsfeld puts it in his Preface, "An act of piety and homage to 80,000 Jews who were victims in France of the persecution of the Nazi era and of its Vichy accomplices." The book was written with the help of his wife, Béate Klarsfeld, who is not Jewish, but who has become a famous Nazi hunter. She helped find Klaus Barbie in South America. The Klarsfelds got much of their information from the Center of the Jewish Documentation in Paris.

When I returned from that Paris trip, I sat down in my office with the French edition of this book. I went over every name, as they were not in alphabetical order. I finally found the names of my father and mother: David and Lydia Zimmern: They were sent to Auschwitz on Convoy No. 40 on November 4, 1942. My father was only forty-six years old, my mother forty-four. I also found the names of my two uncles: My uncle Leopold (Zimmern) was forty-one, my uncle Hugo (Zimmern) forty-four. Hugo was sent to Auschwitz on Convoy No. 18 on August 12, 1942, Leopold on Convoy No. 24 on August 26, 1942. So, within two weeks in 1942, I lost two uncles—and within three months in 1942, I lost my parents and two uncles! Unbelievable! And, I found another name: "Rolf" Zimmern, who was sent on the same convoy as my uncle Hugo: It is very possible he was related to us, but I do not know and may never. I do know, from their letters, that many of our relatives were together in Camp de Gurs—and probably sent to Auschwitz as well.

Most important to me about finding this book and finding the names of my parents and relatives was that I knew, with certainty, they were gone. I was able to place them in time. I could say "Kaddish" for my parents. I knew they were real.

The letters provided another, more intimate, perspective. After having the letters translated by a close friend, Hella Moritz, I could more clearly picture my parents, especially my mother. She appears to have been a very caring person, concerned about others, visiting the sick at Camp de Gurs, and caring about her two babies (my sister and me).

In time, I gathered the strength and—with the encouragement of people close to me—I decided in 1961 to return to Germany to visit Walldürn, where I was born and lived for the first year of my life. When I got there, I mentioned my name to a man in a local shop, said that I had been born there, and that I wanted to see the town by bicycle. He told me to go down a certain street and knock on the door of the woman who rented bicycles.

I did, and showed the woman my passport—and I think she almost passed out. She thought that I was my sister, Béate. She kept saying, "Béate, Béate!" I told her who I was. She ran and looked for someone in the village who knew English. There was one person, the wife of the school principal, who told me that, when the Nazis killed her mother, she had decided to become a Christian. The woman at the bicycle shop explained that her daughter and my sister had played together. She also said that the citizens of the town had had nothing to do with the deportation of the Jews from Walldürn—that it had been the Nazis. They also told me that my parents had been good people.

They showed me the house (even the room) where I was born. (Actually, our house was taken away from our family and been occupied by squatters during and after the war.)

More and more people from the town came to see me. One said that she had delivered milk to our house every morning. And from her, I learned my father had been some type of a salesman.

They prepared a large lunch for me and would not let me stay in the local hotel. I had to stay with them for the night. I asked to see the Jewish cemetery. There, I found my grandmother's grave.

It was as if a celebrity had come to Walldürn. They asked me if I would return. I told them I didn't think so.

In retrospect, thinking about that extraordinary day in Walldürn, I accomplished something for myself: I went back there to find more about my past—and I succeeded. But the price I paid, in emotional and physical anguish, was beyond measure. I had been the only Jewish survivor to return to the place since the war ended!

On April 11, 1983, my husband—Sherman Stokes—accompanied me to Washington, DC, to attend the "American Gathering of Jewish Holocaust Survivors." It was a fantastic experience. I met quite a few survivors from France who had also lived in an OSE children's orphanage. During the Gathering, a survivor came up to me and said he recognized me from the orphanage where I had lived, Taverny. He had a letter that had been signed by a little girl named "Félice" about twenty-three years before. "Well," I said, "that must be me, because there was no one else at Taverny by that name." This person lived in Baltimore and told me not to leave the Gathering until he returned with the letter he had saved all that time. He did. I had written to his adopted family in 1950, thanking them for the donation they had sent to help the group of children at Taverny. But that is another chapter in my life that I cannot recall.

Earlier, I mentioned how I was able to piece together parts of my life using letters written from Camp de Gurs, where my parents and relatives had been interned. My sister and I came into possession of these letters from the same aunt and uncle (who lived in Buffalo) who couldn't take us in when we first came to the United States. But they were among the lucky ones who had been able to emigrate to the States just before the start of the war. In these letters, I was able to read and "hear" the voices of my parents and relatives.

This was the first occasion I had to hear about the conditions in the camp, how terrible it had been in Camp de Gurs. They tell a portion of a story, of one family, crowded, under inhuman conditions, anxiously awaiting their release.

On each piece of letter-paper, numerous correspondents had squeezed in sentences to friends and relatives on the outside—sometimes, my father, my uncles Hugo and Leopold (brothers of my father); at other times, it was my mother and others. They made use of every space on a sheet of paper. Their civility and composure was remarkable, considering the circumstances.

As for me, I pursued my education and received a number of scholarships. I graduated from Stern College in 1966. For more than twenty years I have been working for the Memorial Foundation for Jewish Culture. (I am now retired from the Memorial Foundation, having worked there for forty-four years.)

I was married to a wonderful man—Sherman Stokes—for twenty-five years. He was a compassionate person, very caring, understanding, and supportive. We had a wonderful life together. (Unfortunately, I lost him ten years ago, and he is very much missed.)

In 1970, I submitted to Yad Vashem in Jerusalem the details of the unselfish, life-saving deeds of Mme. Juliette Patoux's heroism. As a consequence, she received a special medal from the Israeli government recognizing her (as well as her husband, Gaston) as a "Righteous Gentile." At the time of her death in France in 1974, her obituary mentioned her recognition as a recipient of this special "Medal of the Just"!

I HAVE ALSO DISCOVERED a few other missing pieces about my parents and my life.

1. Just recently, after I met Béate Klarsfeld, her husband, Serge Klarsfeld, sent me information about my parents' route from Camp de Gurs: They were taken to Camp de Rivesaltes (September 30, 1942) and then to Camp de Drancy (November 4, 1942), and were deported on the same day from there to Auschwitz, where at some point they were gassed.

2. I was taken from Limoges (La Pouponnière), hidden with the Patoux family in the village of La Caillaudière on September 7, 1942, and lived there until November 15, 1945. My sister was brought to the Patouxes during the last months before the war was over. After the liberation, my sister and I were taken to the

orphanage in Draveil; and in October 1947, we were moved to another OSE home, Chateau de Vaucelles in Taverny, where we stayed there until late in January 1951, when we were brought to the States.

3. I also found out through Mr. Klarsfeld the names of some of my other relatives: Anna Zimmern and Henrich Zimmern (both taken to Drancy on May 30, 1944).

4. I have been to many conferences, some for the OSE and Hidden Children meetings, and have made a number of very close friends, because we have shared similar tragic backgrounds. I have stayed in touch with a number of those people.

Bio Note

After she came to the United States on January 31, 1951, Felice Zimmern Stokes went to public school in Newark, New Jersey, and then to Linden High School. Following high school graduation, she enrolled in Stern College (Women's Division of Yeshiva University) in September 1962, and graduated in June 1966.

She worked in several organizations, eventually at the Memorial Foundation for Jewish Culture in New York for forty-four years, from 1966 to 2010, as an executive secretary to the executive vice-president. Since she retired, she has volunteered at a local hospital. She is a member of Congregation Beth Sholom in Teaneck,

New Jersey, where she serves as a member of the board of directors.

She married Sherman Stokes on August 51, 1980, and has two stepchildren, Brian and Claudia. Unfortunately, after twenty-five happy years together, her husband died on September 1, 2005.

As for her sister, she became a nurse and has been married for over fifty years. Béate and her husband, Lenny Michaels, have three children and six grandchildren.

NATHAN'S STORY 1941–42

Clare Ahrens

HE WAS TRANSPORTED from the Mlawa ghetto to Auschwitz in a cattle car crammed to overflowing with other Jews. His group was one of the first to make such a journey. At the entrance to Auschwitz, he could see the words *Arbeit Macht Frei*. His number, with a small triangle beneath it, was tattooed on the inside of his arm and became his new identity. He no longer had a name. Nathan was sixteen years old.

The Nazis had a special plan to enlarge the camp. Under the noses of the Red Cross, Auschwitz-Birkenau was to be built. It was first presented to the Red Cross as a new resettlement center for Jews.

In a humanitarian gesture, it would include a trade school under the auspices of the Red Cross. There, students would learn practical skills such as brick making and bricklaying. The Morter Schuleh, as it was called, would then provide the labor and the know-how to further the construction and development of Auschwitz.

Nathan's good fortune was to be selected as one of these show students.

Indoors, protected from the freezing Polish winter, Nathan survived his first season in hell. As the war escalated, the need to deceive disappeared, and Auschwitz-Birkenau the work camp reverted to what it had always been intended for: the destruction of the Jewish people and other undesirables. The name Auschwitz-Birkenau is synonymous with fear, torment, horror, and death.

It was a place without hope.

Summer 1994

Nathan, my husband, was compelled by our son Richard to return to Poland. Together, we would share the painful memories of Auschwitz and other camps, the loss of family and friends. The small flicker of light not extinguished during the Holocaust years illuminated our journey back, making each of us survivors because of Nathan's courage and heroic example.

Bio Note

Long an American citizen, Claire Ahrens and her husband Nathan live in New York City.

MY STORY AS A HIDDEN CHILD DURING THE HOLOCAUST

Toby Levy

WHEN I LOOKED OUT at the sea of young, innocent faces staring up at me expectantly, instead of the speech I had so carefully prepared I decided to speak from my heart. "You are very lucky you were born here in this wonderful country," I told them. "Appreciate what you have, and don't take any of it for granted. The freedom you have here in America is worth everything." I still couldn't believe that I, an immigrant who was just learning the language and customs of my new country, had been chosen as the valedictorian of my eighth-grade graduating class in New Orleans. How had this happened?

I grew up in Chodorov, a small town in Poland just west of Lviv. My parents, Moshe and Cylia Eisenstein, owned a yard goods store in the "Rynek," the market square. They were well known and respected, and had a reputation for being generous and honest. Life was comfortable. I was six years old and had not yet started school when World War II broke out in 1939. From 1939 until 1941, the Russians occupied the town. Although they confiscated all our valuables, we were still able to remain in our home, and life was bearable.

In June 1941, German soldiers marched down the main street of Chodorov. I still remember their shiny black boots rising and falling in unison as they pounded on the ground. Even at that young age, I knew somehow that it meant the abrupt end of my freedom and childhood. From then on, we lived in constant fear, and food was scarce.

Soon thereafter, the Germans started "resettling" and killing the Jews. To survive, families needed to be lucky, smart enough to plan ahead, and able to get help from others.

One night when my father didn't come home from work, my mother went looking for him and found him in the police station, barely alive. He had been caught bringing a brick home from the lumberyard and had been beaten within an inch of his life. But he survived and, because he did, we also had a chance.

It wasn't long before my father again heard rumors of an impending German *aktion* (mass killing). It was time for the family to go into hiding. My father was a very resourceful and ingenious person. He had been building a fake wall in our cellar for months. He knew one day we would have to hide behind it in order to be safe. The entire family crawled down the small hole he had excavated beneath the cast iron stove, and shut the trap door from the inside. I remember hearing the German boots stomping through our house—those horrible shiny boots—and my grandfather, who was too frail and elderly to crawl into the cellar, being dragged out of his bed. He resisted, saying, "No, shoot me here." Then shots echoed through the house, and we all knew he was gone.

My father put his fingers to his lips, and I knew any sound could be our last as the Germans continued their search. Suddenly, the cellar door opened. I was startled and let out a gasp. "What was that?" I heard a soldier ask. They pounded down the stairs with flashlights on. As I cringed there, I thought, Will they realize that the bricks on one wall look newer than the rest? I held my breath, hoping it would not be my last.

Then we heard a cat's soft meow. One of the soldiers laughed, saying, "Oh, it was just a little black cat. Let's get out of here." With that, they vanished, leaving us in that cellar, shivering in fear but thankful to be still alive. The next day, when we came out of hiding, we found my grandfather dead.

Within a few months, the Germans announced the "relocation" of all Jews to Lviv.

My father's instinct told him the soldiers were lying, and he decided not to follow their orders. He told us we would not leave, and instead started looking for someone to help us. In spite of his reputation, it still took several months to find a place to hide. It was very disheartening. There were nine of us—my grandmother, my parents, my older sister, and my aunt and uncle with their two children. We finally moved into a barn loft belonging to a woman with a teenage son. Her husband had been taken away by the Russians. My father promised to give her everything he owned when the war was over. Her name was Stephania, but we called her "Pritza," our queen, our savior, in Polish.

We hid in the loft most of the day, with little room to move about. For short periods of time, my father would let us stretch our legs down on the barn floor. One day, we were doing that when, all of a sudden, the barn door opened, and there was Pritza. That would have normally been fine, except that a young Ukrainian policeman was behind her. He was checking for hidden Jews in houses and barns. We scrambled behind the hay but still saw the shock on Pritza's face as she thought we had been spotted. She quickly shut the barn door, and we waited in the dark for the soldiers to come. He must not have seen us and only reported that he'd noticed animals in the barn and registered them with the officials in town. Once again, we were lucky to be alive.

After that close call, Pritza was understandably worried for her and her children's safety. She told us we would have to leave. As my father pleaded with her, she responded, "Why don't you try someone else?"

JEWS HAD LIVED IN CHODOROV for hundreds of years, and everyone knew each other. My mom and my aunt went searching for people they knew, but not a single one was willing to take us in. One man said very clearly, "I will pretend I never saw you. Disappear."

After that, we realized we had no place to go. My parents knew it was time to separate and say goodbye. My father told my sister and me that we were going to stay together. My mom said I had to be quiet, obey my sister, and not leave her side. "Always remember who you are. If we don't come back when the war ends, look for Jewish agencies to take you away from this place. Do not let anyone adopt you or convince you to stay here. We have family in the United States and in Palestine."

I was in shock, speechless, and their words made little sense. As an eight-year-old, I did not comprehend the situation fully. I held my sister's hand while my parents kissed us and cried. In the middle of our goodbyes, Tajik, Pritza's sixteen-year-old son, suddenly appeared in the barn. He warned his mother that, if she chased us away, we would surely die. "You are staying here, and I will make you a better hiding place. I will protect you," he reassured us.

WHENEVER I EAT A CHERRY, it immediately brings me back to memories of Tajik. One day he brought us a bowl filled with the delicious fruit from the harvest. He was always there for us with whatever we needed, whether food or protection. One night my uncle wanted to see what time it was and turned on his flashlight to look at his watch. Suddenly, we heard a commotion outside. Tajik immediately came running and told the Germans who had come to inspect that it was his flashlight. Another time a local teenager was prowling around the barn and demanded, "What are you hiding here?"

He answered defiantly, "*Jews*. Do you want to see?"

He was always there for us. That's what I remember. For the next two years, the nine of us hid in the barn's attic. My father kept a sheet of paper on the wall and marked each day, including every Sabbath and Jewish holiday.

The last year of the war, Pritza took in two Germans, for her protection and extra food. That made our lives even more difficult. We were in constant fear and could hardly breathe, knowing that they might hear us. I remember one time Pritza brought us a pound of bread. We had not eaten for days. My father sliced the bread and gave a piece to everyone. My mother cut her portion in half and gave one piece to my sister and the other one to me. This devotion to her children in the face of starvation is a powerful memory that has shaped my future outlook on life.

For three months before we were liberated, Lviv was bombed daily by both the Russians and the British. Pritza and her children had left the house when the bombing started, and she only came from time to time to pick vegetables from the farm. We also took chances to do the same so we wouldn't starve. However, fear had overtaken us. What if the barn's roof was blown off, and we were either killed or, at the very least, discovered? So my father dug a hole in the floor, with a trap door and just enough access for air to breathe. We were hungry, dirty with lice and insects, and had little hope.

One day, under heavy bombardment, we were huddled in the hole when we heard two German soldiers come into the barn. We didn't dare move or even breathe because of the fear of discovery. Since we didn't hear the soldiers leave, we assumed they were lying down in the barn. We sat there quietly for the entire night, and it felt as if we would suffocate.

Finally, we could sit no longer. My father motioned that he would open the trap door and crawl out. If the Germans were there, he would give himself up, so they would take him away and we could survive. He slowly opened the door and looked around.

The Germans had left.

We climbed wearily back up to our hiding place in the loft and slept, secure that, at least that day, we had once again survived.

IN JUNE 1944, WE WERE LIBERATED by the Russians. We came out of our hole and smelled food. However, the Russians told us not to eat and instead find someone who could nurture us back to health. We were lucky again. We found a woman who took us in, gave us a bath, and put us to sleep in a bed with clean, crisp white sheets. She nursed us back to health for the next five weeks, and from then on, we had enough food because my father traded with the Russians.

Bio Note

Toby Levy arrived in New Orleans in 1949 and graduated high school in New York. She also studied in secretarial school for bookkeeping and typing. She worked in Coney Island Hospital for twenty years, until her husband became ill with Parkinson's disease, and when he could no longer travel to the city, she had to take over his jewelry business.

They have two children, a son, Dr. Howard J. Levy, an orthopedic surgeon; and a daughter, Myra, who is an occupational therapist. Presently, although Toby still continues with the jewelry business, she is a docent at the Museum of Jewish Heritage, a Living Memorial to the

Holocaust, lectures in schools, and volunteers in the Israeli Army once a year. She is also on the board of her synagogue and lives a very productive and fulfilling life.

THE BORROWED CHILD[1]

Lola Bielski Dzienciolski Kline
and Bella Bielski Dzienciolski Rubin

IT WAS JULY 1944. The war was still raging in Europe, but the Nazis were retreating. The Red Army had liberated many partisans in eastern Poland (Belarus of today), including the Bielski Brothers Otriad, in the largest Jewish family partisan camp in Poland.[2]

My parents, Taiba Bielski Dzienciolski and Avremel Dzienciolski, along with many other partisans, walked out of the woods, the Naliboka *puscha*, alive and well. There was only one thing on their

---

[1] The title is from a chapter in *Painless Vocabulary* by Michael Greenberg, p. 257.
[2] Tec, 1993; and Duffy, 2003.

minds: their baby girl, Lodje.

Lodje, as she was then called, was being cared for by a childless Polish couple. They had promised to reunite her with her biological parents if they survived the war. Now it was time. They were obsessed with getting their child back. Taiba dreamed of holding her in her arms again. Lodje had been only nine months old when they left her with these foster parents. They had suffered enough—three years in the forests with little food and almost no hope for the future. But it had made them strong, if only because of one thought: seeing their baby girl again.

The above story was one of many such scenarios. In Poland in 1939, there had been more than one million Jewish children. Only about 5,000 survived by the end of the war.[3] Many of these children had been hidden by kindly people in secret places—in churches, cellars, attics, village chicken coops, barns, and other hiding spots. Some of them were not even aware of their Jewish identities. I was one of these hidden children, and this is my story.

I KNEW NOTHING ABOUT my biological parents. I was almost four years old at the end of the war, living in a

---

[3] Website of the American-Israeli Cooperative Enterprise, 2014.

house in the countryside in the village of Huta Scklana, in the area of Baranovich in eastern Poland, the Belarus, as I have said, of today, speaking Polish to my "adoptive" parents, wearing a cross and saying prayers at night like a good little Catholic girl, innocently believing that I was safe and sound at home with my mother and father.

Little did I know that my real parents had made a deal with an elderly childless couple who had agreed to take care of me as their own. After I was safely hidden, my parents were able to remain in the forest (until they were liberated) with the Bielski family partisan group, which at first consisted mainly of my mother's brothers, Tuvia, Zus, Asael, and Aaron, my parents, and a few other family members, my father's brother Shleme Dzienciolski, my aunt Haya, my cousin Pinek Boldo, and some others. Our small family group fled into the forests, hoping to defy the Nazis by staying alive and even fighting back as armed partisans. Their initially meager camp grew into the largest Jewish family partisan group in Poland. Approximately 1,200 Jews survived there, due largely to the leadership of Tuvia Bielski, the commander, and his brothers, and to the tenacity of their families and friends, who were determined not to give up their freedom and to survive the war.

My Story

I'm going to move forward towards the end of my story because that was the most traumatic part for me. What happened profoundly affected the rest of my life.

After surviving the war, my biological parents were forced to "abduct" me from the couple I had always assumed were my parents, because they refused to give me up.

As prearranged in a manner I knew nothing about, one cloudy afternoon, my biological parents showed up in Huta Scklana, where I was living at the time. They were accompanied by a man whom I later discovered was a government official.

They spoke to some adults who were standing around. Then two of these strangers came over to us, the children, who were sitting in a circle, playing a game. They asked in Polish, "Which one of you is Lodje Kenceizier?"

One young girl spoke up, pointed to me, and said, "She is." (In 1993, when I revisited Belarus, I met a man named Victor who told me he remembered that moment, and that it was his elder sister who had pointed me out. Victor was still living in the same house where I had been hidden, but by then he had a wife and four children.)

The strangers walked up to me and asked me in Polish if I was really Lodje Kenceizier. I nodded. Then they asked, "Do you know the way to Novogrudek?" Of course I said yes. They pretended to look confused and asked me to walk them down a road. They again asked if that was the way to Novogrudek, and did I know where the turn to town was. To me it seemed obvious where it was, but they still seemed confused and again asked about the turn. They then asked me to ride with them in the wagon until we reached the turn. I was offered a bag of candy as a bribe. (In those days candy was a precious gift.)

They promised to let me out of the wagon at the corner.

Of course, this never happened. I got the candy but was never allowed out of the wagon. I became hysterical, began pounding on them, crying, and trying to get out.

That was the end of my so-called happy childhood with the people I called Mama and Papa, the Kenceiziers.

The neighbors didn't interfere. They even encouraged me to go along with these strangers. I later found out they had been told that the Kenceiziers would be away for a few days, and someone would come to take me to them. In fact, through bribes, this part of the story was also prearranged by my father. He had managed to have Mr. Kenceizier recruited into the army, but the entire military service call-up was a sham since Mr. Kenceizier was too old to serve. With him being away and his wife going to visit him, my biological parents had the opportunity to come and get me.

The trauma of being "abducted" from my adoptive parents stayed with me for many years, manifesting itself in different ways. One of the effects of this early childhood experience was my mistrust of people, and as a result, the difficulties I often had maintaining certain relationships, especially with my parents.

The Beginning: The Dzienciolskis and the Bielskis

I was born in the village of Big Izvah near Novogrudek. Novogrudek was later incorporated into Russia and is today part of Belarus. The land in Big Izvah belonged to my father's family, the Dzienciolskis, my Babe Idke and my Zede Aaron. They owned a mill, and people came from all over the area to grind their wheat into flour. The mill did quite well, and my grandparents were prosperous. They even employed workers from the local Polish population. In fact, they did so well that their home had wooden floors, a sign that showed that they were rising in the community. Wooden floors were a status symbol in a rather class-conscious society, where most people's homes had dirt floors. My mother, Taibe, was a Bielski from the village of Stankevich, and when she married Avremel, she became a Dzienciolski. Both my parents remained living on the Dzienciolski land with my grandparents until just after the Nazis came and destroyed everything.

Taking Refuge in the Forest

In June 1941, the Luftwaffe began bombing eastern Poland, including Novogrudek and the surrounding villages.[4] Later the German army arrived, and the notorious persecution and slaughter of Jews began. Toward the end of 1941, German soldiers arrived in Stankevich and, together with Polish policemen, eventually made their way to the homestead of my Bielski grandparents, Beyla and David. As they were being rounded up to be taken to the killing fields and murdered, my youngest Bielski uncle, Archik (Aaron), unnoticed, was hiding behind a tree at the far end of the property closer to the forest. He watched in horror while his parents were being forced out of their home

---

[4] Duffy, p. 31.

and pushed into an open truck. Archik escaped, found his elder Bielski brothers, Zus and Asael, and told them what had happened. They in turn sent him to the Dzienciolski household to tell Taibe, their sister and my mother, to leave immediately and follow him to the Bielski hideout deep inside the woods.

When Archik reached my mother's house, he yelled, "Taibe! The Nazis are rounding up the Jews in the area. Our parents are gone! You have to get out of here right away! Our brothers and Avremel are waiting for you in the forest. Hurry!"

My mother grabbed me, covered me with a blanket, took nothing else with her, and, along with other family members, ran after her youngest brother into the forest.

I WAS ABOUT THREE MONTHS OLD when the Nazis invaded Novogrudek and started their heinous programs against the Jews, and about six months old when the mass killings started and my parents took refuge in the forest. Conditions there were very primitive. We had little food and shelter. I was cold and hungry, and soon became sick. My crying jeopardized the safety of the small family group since "a crying infant could draw unwanted attention from German soldiers [or Polish police and other Nazi collaborators] . . . who were on the lookout for Jews in hiding."[5]

Something had to be done, and it had to be done quickly. My parents were desperate. They had to find a home for me.

How I Became a Hidden Child

Through my father and his connections, a childless older Polish couple was found. The man had previously worked in the mill on the Dzienciolski land. A deal was struck between my father and Mr. Kenceizier and his wife to take me in as their own. Food and money would be supplied by my parents, and my Jewish identity would be concealed. The couple promised to return me to my parents if they survived the war. If they did not survive, the Kenceiziers could keep me as their own child, and I would go on living the life of a little peasant girl. That was the arrangement. My mother put a cross around my neck and pinned a note to my blanket that said the following:

> *I am a Christian baby born to a poor family. Because of the war my family cannot take care of me any longer. I am begging anyone that finds me to please take me home and take care of me.*

---
[5] Greenberg, p. 259.

On a cold wintry night, my father, his brother Shleme, and my uncle Zus Bielski and cousin Pinek Bolda (who was only about sixteen years old at the time) placed me on a snow bank under a window at the home of the Kenceiziers. My mother was not present at the time, because everyone felt that she would be too traumatized by the act of giving me away.

The men then hid behind a mound of snow across the street and waited quietly to see what would happen next. Time passed. I wriggled out of my blanket, felt the sting of the cold air, and started crying. After a while, the door opened and Mrs. Kenceizier came outside to investigate. She saw me, picked me up, and brought me into her warm home to show her husband what she had found. From that moment, I began living with my adoptive parents; my name became Lodje Kenceizier, and my Jewishness began to fade. After witnessing this intense event, my father and the other family members found their way back into the dense forest.

Many years later, I would learn how difficult it was for my parents to give me away, not knowing if they would ever see me again.

After examining me thoroughly, to avert suspicion the Kenceiziers decided to take me to the local police station the next day to report that they had found an abandoned baby. The couple pleaded with the police chief to allow them to keep this found infant because they didn't have any children of their own and they believed I was a gift from God. The police chief accepted their version of the story and gave in to their request. It was fortunate that this incident was brought to his attention, because on two subsequent occasions, neighbors complained that there was a Jewish child hidden in their neighbor's home. We were called to the police station twice more, and each time the situation was reexamined. My adoptive parents were questioned, and in fact, at one point, because I smiled at the police chief and grabbed onto his finger, he contemplated taking me home to his wife. However, the case was closed on the second visit. The police chief remarked that he had dealt with this situation previously; I was not a Jewish child and my adoptive parents could keep me.

The case would be closed forever. My fate would have been doomed if not for my parents' well-thought out, convincing plan, and the kindness of my adoptive parents.

Living with the Kenceiziers: A Few Recollections

When I became too big for a crib (by then I had been living with my adoptive parents for several months), my parents moved me into a bed. However, because there was intermittent bombing and shooting going on, they made use of the crib by putting straw into it and positioning it in front of our window, so that we could lie flat on the floor in front of it to protect ourselves from periodic shooting. My adoptive parents placed me between them and put their arms around me for protection. There we lay until the shooting incidents ended.

Potty Training

In my small child's recollection, we had a wooden kitchen table, and our bathroom, the outhouse, was located in our yard, close to the edge of our property. This presented a problem with my potty training, so my adoptive mother placed the potty on the kitchen table and sat me on the potty while my father stood beside her, gently patting my head. My mother spoke little endearments to me, kissed my knees and encouraged me to go. . . . It worked.

Feelings of Terror

They were bombing us. Planes flew over my head, and I ran home to my parents for protection. Afterwards they brought me outside, pointed to the barn, and told me not to go there. Since I was a small child, I didn't heed their warning; I was curious about the barn and why it looked so damaged. I had to go there and investigate for myself. Later, when I was all alone, I walked over. There were wooden planks and stones strewn around, and I stepped cautiously over everything and entered the collapsed barn. Then I came to a big deep hole in the ground. I gazed down but became so frightened that I immediately stepped back. Years later, when I was living in the U.S., I had horrible nightmares about this incident. In those dreams I imagined seeing dozens of snakes slithering around at the bottom of the hole and me leaning over about to fall in.

Shiny Black German Boots

Shiny black knee-high army boots were another of my terrors. My adoptive parents always warned me against the Nazis. They constantly told me not to speak to them or engage them. I was to stay as far away as possible when I saw them. In fact, the German soldiers would periodically come to our building, looking for Jews. They would bang on each apartment door with their rifle butts and shout in their harsh German, "Are there any Jews here? Do you know of anyone harboring Jews?"

As we heard them shouting and banging, we sat in fear until they came to our door. The banging itself was enough to scare me half to death, so when they came, my adoptive parents would make me stand back and warn me again not to speak. Then my adoptive father would open the door, and I, short as I was, stood there with downcast eyes looking at the shiny black knee-high boots. I became so terrified of those boots that I carried those memories with me for many years. My terror nights would vacillate between the memory of the bombed-out barn and its snakes and those boots.

Living with My Biological Parents

As I described above (in "My Story"), my biological parents abducted me from my adoptive parents after they left their hiding place in the forest. The following is an account of what it was like those first few months after being reunited with my real parents.

Building a Church

We were living at a relative's home in Novogrudek after my parents left the forest. In the beginning, I was so desperate to go to pray each time I heard church bells that I finally built a little altar of my own in the corner of our small room. It consisted of a makeshift Mother Mary sitting on a cloth surrounded by candles. I would kneel there whenever I felt I needed comforting, and I would pray to my God.

Occasionally, I would build a secret home for myself—a kind of hideaway under the kitchen table, which was often covered by a mid-length tablecloth. I felt safe there. I pretended I was back home with my adoptive Polish parents and not with "those ugly, smelly, bearded Jews." I called my real parents' names and uttered the anti-Semitic slurs I had often heard spoken by people around me while living with my adoptive parents.

Going to Church

One Sunday, the bells were ringing, and I became hysterical. I was accustomed to going to church, and I wanted to. After all, I had received my First Communion in the Catholic faith. I remember that day specifically, because I wore a beautiful white satin-and-lace dress with white socks and shoes, and walked down the aisle, following other young girls, holding flowers and feeling very beautiful and very proud.

My biological parents had no way of comforting me when I heard these church bells and insisted on going to church. They had never been in a church. They did not understand what went on in one. In fact, as Jews, they were forbidden to enter a church and thought it was a sin.

My mother's cousin Essie, only eighteen at the time, had noticed me praying at my makeshift altar and became concerned about my outbursts. She approached my mother and asked if she could take me to church. My mother gave her permission, and on a later Sunday, when the situation reoccurred, Essie took me by the hand and walked me to the local Novogrudek church.

We went inside. I was immediately relieved, and she allowed me to recite my prayers. Later she walked me over to a blue-and-white statue of Mother Mary holding little baby Jesus in her arms, illuminated by small lit candles. I gazed up at the Virgin Mary and felt content at that moment, but Essie put her hand on the statue and said to me, "Why are you praying to her? This is only a fake figure made of clay, and it means nothing." Being a little girl, I had no response, but I found myself thinking about those words and, actually, after that, don't remember ever again asking to be taken to church.

Hitchhiking

Once I tried to get back to my adoptive parents. I dressed myself in typical Polish style, put on a *chustka* (kerchief) and a shawl around my shoulders, then stood on a busy corner, trying to hitch a ride. Someone spotted me and asked, "What are you doing here?"

I answered, "I'm going to my parents, of course!" When I was asked how I was going to get there, I replied, "I'll stop a passing truck driver who'll take me home."

The next question was, "But how will you pay him?"

I said, "My father will give him a bottle of vodka."

Knock on the Door

There was a soft knock on the door. I don't remember who, but someone opened it. In great distress my mother grabbed me off the floor, threw a blanket over me, and ran out the back way. She rushed down a path fenced in on both sides and through a gate into a neighbor's apartment. I had no idea why she seemed so frightened and why the two of us had departed so suddenly.

Several days later, this scene repeated itself, but this time Essie opened the door, and I was amazed to see my adoptive parents standing there. Boy, was I happy! I ran toward my adoptive father, grabbed him, and wouldn't let go. He pulled me into his arms and started kissing me. I put my arms around his neck, squeezed tight, and cried with delight. My biological mother tried to pull me out of his arms. I grabbed his ears, because I was being pulled away, and held on even tighter. I just couldn't and wouldn't let go of those ears. I became hysterical, and only by sheer force was I finally pulled away and dragged to a neighbor's apartment. The worst had come true. I was once again separated from those whom I loved and thought were my real parents.

My biological parents and my adoptive parents must have come to some understanding, because after that incident, my adoptive mother would come and spend nights with me. She would hold me in her arms and comfort me. I was so happy then, sleeping contentedly in her arms, holding her and never wanting anything more than that comfort. I couldn't think beyond those moments, her arms around me as I snuggled against her. That was a feeling of security and peace.

However, this arrangement troubled my real mother, who feared that the Poles would run off with me, so when it came time to leave Poland, they left without saying good-bye to them or to anyone else.

Escape to the West

Rumors filtered through that the borders were about to close as the Red Army took more control of the area. My parents decided to flee. Late one night, under cover of darkness, we left Novogrudek. Through bribes and forged travel papers that were prepared for us by cousin Essie's husband, Jerry, we boarded a train for Germany and eventually ended up in a displaced persons camp called Fahrenwald, in Bavaria. The camp was under the protection of the Allied forces, mainly the Americans. There we remained for around three years, until my uncle Walter Bell—the oldest of the Bielski children, who had been living in the U.S. before the war—found us and, late in 1948, arranged for our immigration to America.

And here is where I have remained. It was quite difficult for me and my family to adjust to life in America. First of all, my name became Lola. I could not speak the language, the customs were different, and my family and I even looked different. We dressed differently—I had never seen children who wore socks and shoes that matched their clothes, and I'd never seen so much good food. Also, children in my part of the world had never argued with their parents in public. It was considered bad manners to contradict or raise your voice to an elder, especially a parent.

My parents were damaged by the war as well. They were afraid of anything that had to do with the government, the police, or some other authority. They were untrusting of anyone outside the family. They were afraid that, if they did anything wrong, they might get sent back to the horrible world from which they had come, even be taken to jail. They wanted desperately to blend into the American way of life and be considered Americans themselves. Because of their fears, I, too, became afraid and untrusting, and I had a hard time coping with the world around me. I continued to have nightmares about the war, the Germans, and the horrible things they might do to me if they caught me.

Despite my hardships in adjusting to a new life, I went to school, married, had two wonderful children,

Jacee and Jeff, and later divorced my husband after twenty years of marriage. While married, one of the things that became a constant source of irritation was my husband's negative attitude toward my family, specifically my Bielski uncles. While I admired them and considered them heroes who had saved over 1,200 Jews, including not only armed Jewish fighters but also women, children, and the elderly, my husband had a lack of interest in their lives and even a distaste for them. This manifested itself in several ways, one of which being his growing disinterest in coming to family functions. Another was his belief that they had not done anything heroic and significant during the war, reflected in remarks like the following: "I don't understand why you think your uncles are so great. They didn't do anything. It was mainly luck that they survived. Your family is not so great, and your uncles did what everyone else did—they tried to survive."

Now, in my later years, I look back on my past as a dream that happened long ago to someone I hardly remember. After turning forty, I started to accept my damaged past. I became more independent, more confident in my decision-making. I also attended the first International Hidden Child Conference held in Manhattan in June 1991, which resulted in me joining a support group of hidden children sponsored by the Hidden Child Foundation/ADL.

I worked, retired, raised my children, and now they are raising theirs. My daughter, Jacee, has three children—Brianna, and the twins, Jake and Jared. My son, Jeff, and his wife Sarah, have two children, William Taz (named after my uncles Tuvia, Asael, and Zus) and Sam. My sister Bella, who was born in the Fahrenwald DP camp, is a widow and lives in Israel with her two sons. My sister Charlotte, and her husband, Michael, also have two children and live in Manhattan.

The story of the Bielski brothers eventually came to the attention of Hollywood, resulting in the 2008 Paramount Vantage movie *Defiance*, directed by Edward Zwick. It has been translated into several languages and is still being screened in many countries and at Holocaust memorial events.

Acknowledgments

I would like to thank Michael Greenberg for contributing his comments on an earlier version of this memoir. We are also grateful to the Hidden Child Foundation/ADL for supporting the publication of this work.

Note: Some of the details describing events and

dates in this account may differ slightly from previous documentation, as witnesses often viewed them from different perspectives.

References

American-Israeli Cooperative Enterprise, 2014. *Aiww.jewishvirtuallibrary.org/jsource/Holocaust/hidden.html.*

Duffy, Peter, 2003. *The Bielski Brothers.* HarperCollins Publishers Inc., New York.

Greenberg, Michael, 2006. "The Borrowed Child." *Painless Vocabulary.* Barron's Educational Series, Inc., New York, pp. 257-260.

Tec, Nechama, 1993. *Defiance, The Bielski Partisans.* New York: Oxford University Press.

Bio Note

After the war Lola Kline's family spent several years in the Fahrenwald Displaced Persons' Camp in Germany. They arrived in the United States in 1949, and she started school in the third grade. She graduated from high school in 1959 but continued her education with an associate of arts degree in later years.

She married, had two children, and now has five grandchildren. After she retired from work and because of her hidden child background, she became involved with New Jersey's Department of Children and Families and took in several foster children. This was her "give-back" for being a foster child herself. Also, in 1993 members of her family and she took a trip to a section of Belarus that had formerly been part of Poland, in search of their family roots. She met several Poles who had known her family before and during the war, and she even met a man who had been a child during the war and remembered her as one of his playmates. This was an extremely emotional moment for her. He still lives in the same house their families shared so many years ago.

In 2008 Paramount produced a film called *Defiance*, which chronicled the exploits of Bielski's family during the Holocaust. The film brought new attention to her family's history and caused her to reflect anew on her own experiences during that period.

MY BROTHER, GÜNTHER

Carl Hausman

THE YEAR WAS 1939 in Hitler's Germany. My brother, Günther, and I were already in the crosshairs of the Nazis.

Günther, who was four years older than me, had attended public school in the small town of Kirchheimbolanden, located near the Black Forest region where our family lived.

At age six it was my turn to start school. Jewish children were no longer allowed to attend the public schools. My brother and I had to travel by train to another town, where a Jewish school was located. The children in our town amused themselves by pelting us with stones and insults daily as we got off the train. Günther was my sole shield and protector during those horrific events in my young life.

I was ten years old in 1940 when our family was deported from our home to concentration camps in the south of France. In the years following our deportation, we were all separated. Günther, who had been my constant companion and protector, was lost to me forever. We were to be removed from the camp for our safety, but, not wanting to be separated from my mother, I was unable to join him.

I survived the Holocaust. He did not!

My brother, Günther. My great protector from the Nazi stones and insults.

I will miss him all the days of my life.

In 1941 Günther was sent to a Christian orphanage near the city of Toulouse. I remained in the Camp de Gurs with my parents. When he became of age, a Jewish congregation in that city helped him to have a Bar Mitzvah.

In the same year, 1942, he was old enough to visit my parents, who had been transferred to another camp, Rivesaltes.

I had been removed from there by the Jewish organization OSE to a children's home in St. Raphael.

On September 4, 1942, I received a postcard from Günther, mailed from the camp where he had joined my parents, telling me that they were going to again be moved.

Many years later I learned from a book by Serge Klarsfeld that my family had been shipped in cattle cars to Drancy near Paris, and from there to Auschwitz on Transport No. 31 on September 11, 1942, with a thousand other Jews. All of them were gassed upon their arrival.

Bio Note

Carl Hausman was hidden by families in France until the end of the war. He came to the United States in 1947. In 2007 he published his memoir, *Rescued: The Story of a Child Survivor of the Holocaust in France,* which was translated to German.

Lola Kline with her parents, Farhrenwald, Germany

Lola Kline and her mother, Farhrenwald, Germany

Lola Kline with her father, Fahrenwald, Germany

Günther (left) and Carl Hausman with their mother, Carolina

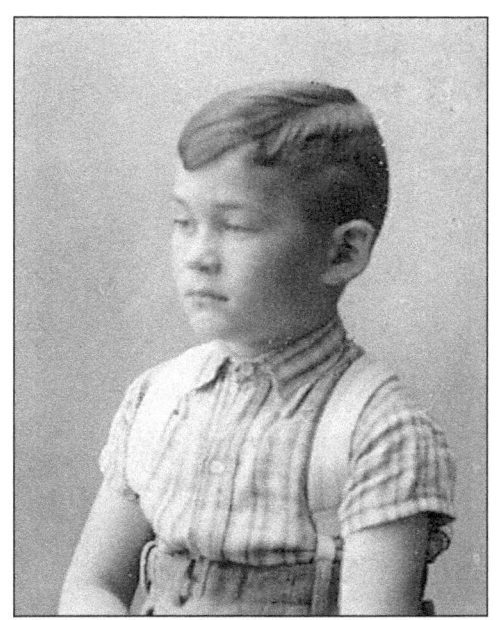

Carl Hausman

Carl (left) and Günther Hausman

Felice Zimmern Stokes, left, and her sister, Béate

Felice Zimmern Stokes with Mme. Patoux

Felice Zimmern Stokes (first row, first on left), sitting next to her sister, Béate, with their counselor, Hélène, at Taverny

Susan Gold, Age 4

Susan Gold, Age 4

Toby Eisenstein Levy, 1944–1945

Toby Eisenstein Levy with her sister and mother

Toby Eisenstein Levy and her sister

Ruth Gruener

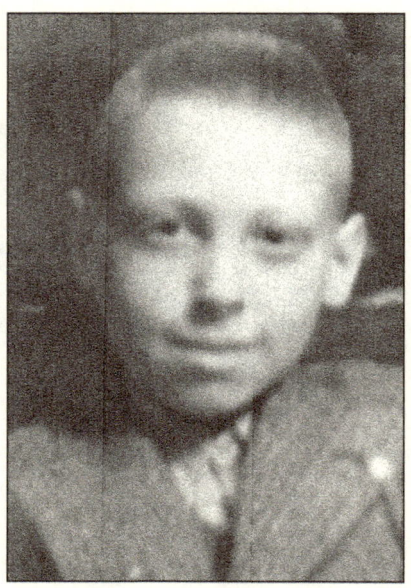

Charles Roman, who left Austria in 1938 and reached Paris in 1939 in the same jacket

Charles Roman (second row, third from left), kindergarten, Austria, Summer 1931

Judy Gertler

Essie Shor (left), and her partisan comrade Itka, with whom she went on missions, 1944

Danielle Lerman

Danielle Lerman

Helga Shepard

Zahava Szàsz Stessel

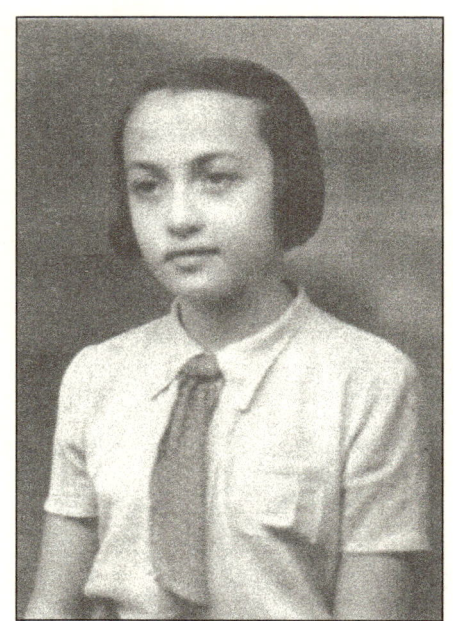

Rina Nudel

Rina and her brother Hesio, Bucharest, 1944

MY WAR YEARS HISTORY

Charles Roman

I WAS BORN IN VIENNA. My parents were divorced, and my mother had to work very hard to earn a living. She was employed by a Jewish lawyer but lost her job after Germany annexed Austria in 1938 and the racial laws were implemented. I was eleven years old.

I went to public school and was promptly sent to the back of the class, totally ignored, as if I were a speck of dust. Eventually, I was thrown out of school and sent to a segregated school for Jews only. Every day when school let out, a mob gathered in front; we were spat on, insulted, and screamed at, our clothing torn. At that point, I refused to go to school and became a truant.

So we had to flee Austria. It was impossible to obtain visas to other countries, so we tried to slip illegally into Switzerland, Luxembourg, and France, but we were caught every time and sent back to Germany.

Out of money and with no place to go, we returned to Vienna, where we still had our apartment. Then came November 10, *Kristallnacht*, the night of broken glass. After that, we tried a second time to enter France illegally.

We were caught once more in Strasbourg. This time, we were taken to police headquarters, and everything was conducted in French. I only knew German and had no idea what was going on. Then I was taken to a hospital ward for abandoned children and guarded by Catholic nuns.

And there I was—no mother or father, and no language. I was desperate to know what had happened to my mother. After three long weeks, a woman from the Jewish community finally came and told me my mother had been sent to prison for a month for illegally crossing the border, and that we had to return to Germany at the end of her sentence.

Instead of leaving, we took a train to Paris and extended our stay until the war broke out and they could not send us back to Germany.

I went to school in Paris and learned French very quickly. In November 1939, I was evacuated to a children's home in the center of France, near Limoges, run by the OSE, Oeuvres de Secours aux Enfants. These were chateaux converted into living quarters for children. There was a documentary made of the story called *The Children of Chabannes*. I am one of them. Later I was transferred to another home called Montintin.

In August 1942, the French police came to the children's home, arrested me, and brought me to the camp of Rivesaltes in southwestern France, where the deportation trains were formed. My father was deported from Belgium to Rivesaltes. At the roll call to go on the cattle car, he answered for himself and me. But I remained at the landing and did not get on the train. At the end of the roll call, a few people were left. When they asked for my name, I said "Rosenberg." It was not on the list, so I was sent back to camp for the next transport.

A Red Cross worker there, a former educator at Chabannes, recognized me and smuggled me out in a Red Cross car. They removed the rear seat, under which the tools to repair flat tires were normally kept.

I was squeezed under that seat, and people took seats on top of me. This is how I escaped.

I returned to the home I had been taken from and was given false ID as a French citizen, with which I joined a youth organization, Compagnions de France, a sort of paramilitary organization for the then ruler Maréchal Pétain.

One day I was called to the chief's office and asked a lot of questions about my background. I got scared and went AWOL—in other words, ran away without travel documents, a must . . . but my uniform got me by. I went to where my mother was staying in forced residence in an isolated French village in the Italian-occupied zone. The Italians did not enforce the racial laws to any great extent and treated us like any other enemy aliens.

We were in this isolated mountain village in the French Alps called St. Martin Vésubie. On September 8, 1943, the Italians capitulated and returned to Italy. At first they took us with them. We were about a thousand Jews; but they abandoned us in the middle of nowhere, so we continued on foot over a mountain pass about eight thousand feet high. There were no roads or footpaths, only rocks and stones. We simply followed the people in front of us. My mother said,

"This is like the Exodus out of Egypt, like in the Bible." She and I took some photographs of the crossing of the Alps. These pictures, the only evidence in existence of that journey, now reside in the Holocaust museums in Washington, Milan, and Paris.

After three days of walking and climbing, we reached the village of Valdieri, in Italy. We had expected the Allies to occupy all of Italy, but instead the Germans did. A few days later, an order was posted in the town square that all foreigners had to present themselves in that square. Those who obeyed the order were quickly surrounded by SS and Italian soldiers, marched to the next town, Borgo San Dalmazzo, and from there deported to Auschwitz.

My mother and I did not go but snuck out a back door and fled into the mountains. So did others, as well as Italian soldiers who had not returned to their units and were now deserters.

We stayed high up in a mountain church until November 1943. It got too cold and windy to remain there after that, so we moved to the next valley, on the sunny side, in places where the farmers kept their tools for work during the summer.

We had no water, no food or sanitation, only four stone walls. We did get some help from the local farmers, who permitted us to use their premises to hide in, offered us food, and let us use the blankets that the cows used during the day when they left the barn. We picked them up in the evening, carried them up to our hideout, and returned them at daybreak for the cows to use again.

My mother, who was very resourceful, transformed old discarded garments into useful wear—like a man's suit into a jacket and skirt—entirely by hand. She had no sewing machine. There was no electricity, water, or sanitation. We chopped wood and burned it in a chimney to keep warm. She also knitted me a sweater and a hat out of old sweaters that had been discarded (I still have the hat!).

My mother and I remained there until March 1944 and then made our way to Rome. Again we had forged documents to travel on. As we made our way south by train, the tracks were bombed out by the Allies. We eventually reached Florence, where we narrowly escaped being arrested. We continued south to Orvieto, again bombed by the Allies. There were no more trains from there on, so we hitchhiked in German army trucks, and I soon became the interpreter between three Italian girls and three German soldiers.

Eventually we got to Rome, and the three soldiers

went off to the front near Monte Cassino.

We hid in Rome until liberation by the Allies in June 1944. I came to the United States in November 1949. Eleven months later, I was drafted into the American Army and was very proud to be an American soldier. I also served some time in Korea.

Note:

There is a documentary about the St. Martin Vésubie episode entitled *A Pause in the Holocaust*.

Bio Note

Charles Roman was liberated in Rome, Italy, in June 1944, and remained there for five years, working for the American Joint Distribution Committee. In 1949, he immigrated to the United States, where he worked in a factory. He was drafted into the army in 1951 and was sent to Korea as a field radio repairman. When he returned in 1953, he opened his own business in sales and service for TV and air-conditioning. He married in 1955. He and his wife, Inge, have a daughter and two grandchildren.

HAVE U.S. PASSPORT—
WILL IT SAVE ME?

Judith Gertler

It was mid-December 1944 when the Jews of Munkacs, Hungary, were obliged to leave the ghetto on foot for an ancient fort on the outskirts of Komarom. It had been built in the form of a star and was called "Csillag Eröd," which means "Star Fort."

The place wore the battle scars of many centuries. The weather was horrendous. The roads were icy and slushy with snow and sleet all the way during our death march from Budapest. With feet frozen, and dead tired, we were ushered into a huge labyrinth with no windows or electric lights, actually the basement storage area for animal feed.

There was some straw spread on the cement floor. We collapsed into this space, in wet clothing, close to one another, for warmth. Next to the door two pails were provided—one for drinking water and another for our hygienic needs. We had no belongings, as we had dropped everything on the long way, to be able to keep up with the march. Our guards, members of the Hungarian Arrow-Cross (*nyilas*) Party, chased us with their dogs and rifles toward the German border.

Prior to what would for some be a death march, our group had been kept under the protection of the Swiss consul, hoping to be exchanged for war prisoners. Then one day they had collected all the prison inmates in the city, and we were attached to that unholy transport called the *tolonc* (vagrants).

The language and the behavior of these people, some of whom were ordinary criminals, were shocking to my innocent ears. They were brutal, angry, and abusive people. I clung to my aunt, Mariska, and couldn't get my thoughts together.

My mother had been with us till the night before, and now she was missing. She had not reached our stopping place in the fortress of Komarom. I looked for her and asked my aunt how they had become separated. I myself had not been with them at the time, since the guards had taken children out of the line and placed us in carts.

My aunt explained that my mother had been unable to keep up and had lagged behind. The Arrow Cross guards urged those who walked badly to rest by the road. The *nyilas* reassured the ones who had given up that, just like the children, they too would be picked up by carts.

The one that I was placed in was at the end of the column, and I noticed the people who couldn't keep up were being escorted toward the bushes and shot in the back. I couldn't imagine that my mother might have been among them. I was hoping that she was in a cart and I waited anxiously for her arrival.

Days passed while we stayed in that dark fortress. Then December 20, 1944, my eleventh birthday, I became so distraught that I demanded an explanation from my aunt of why she had not held on to my mother.

How could she answer me?

IN THE GHETTO OF MUNKACS, my mother had saved me from deportation to Auschwitz. She was a U.S. citizen with a valid passport, and that gave us the opportunity to be protected by the Swiss consulate. My aunt, who had been living in Budapest, was also with us.

When she was young, my mother had emigrated to the U.S. and lived in New York for eleven years. When the Depression came, she had lost her job and decided to visit her family in Munkacs, which at that time was part of Czechoslovakia, and later returned to Hungary. Upon arriving she was introduced to a handsome, eligible young man. Love conquered her desire to return to the U.S.

When the war broke out, my mother's first thought was to return to New York. The American consul advised her to purchase the tickets and leave Europe immediately. We sold our home, shipped some of our belongings, and gave Grandma the furniture. Meanwhile, there were changes in the immigration laws, the latest of which decreed that my mother could leave immediately, but that her child and husband would have to wait three months before being able to follow. She had been unable to commit herself to that separation. Thus, we remained trapped in the war with the rest of the Jews of Munkacs.

We waited in the fortress of Csillag Eröd until the German trains became available. Then we were transported to Ravensbrück, a camp inside Germany. We got there on January 7, 1945. For months we suffered the atrocities and brutality of a concentration camp, and before our final liberation we had to endure a second forced march.

What an irony of fate that, after my mother and I became separated, the American passport that had been sewn into the lining of my coat was taken from me upon arrival at the camp, marking the end of U.S. protection for me and leaving me with only the memory of my mother.

Bio Note

Judith Gertler came to the United States in 1957, after which she took a course in beauty culture. After she married Harry Gertler and her son graduated from high school, she entered Touro College in New York City and graduated with a B.A. in Social Studies. Her activities include NAHOS, the Hidden Child group, and the book club. Her son is now a successful lawyer, and she is thrilled to have three amazing grandchildren.

HOW ACTS OF KINDNESS SAVED LIVES—MINE AND MY PARENTS'

Ruth Gruener

Though the Holocaust occurred decades ago, I just found out a few months ago how my story came about.

I was born in Lvov, Poland, where my parents had a shop in which they made chocolates, some hand-dipped, hard candy, ice cream, and French pastries. The business did very well. They had many loyal customers. Some became good friends.

My father was assigned by the Nazis to a job outside the ghetto. One evening, upon coming back from work, he told me and my mom that something very special had happened to him outside the ghetto going to work.

"I noticed Mrs. Sczygiel," he said. She was one of our customers. She stopped me and said, 'I assume that you, your wife, and your child will be killed. I want to save the life of your little girl. Tomorrow, bring her out of the ghetto and take her to the place where you work. I will come, pick her up, and take her to my house.'"

The next morning I left the ghetto with my dad, hidden under his long winter coat. Mrs. Sczygiel picked me up and took me to her apartment, where she lived with her mother, husband, and three young daughters.

A few weeks later, my father, while walking to his job, met Mr. Oyak, the pastry baker who had worked in my parents' shop. He told Mr. Oyak that I was being hidden by the Sczygiel family and hopefully would survive the war. He told Mr. Oyak, "I would so much want my daughter to have a mother! Maybe you and your wife could hide my wife?" Mr. Oyak answered that my parents were not only his bosses but very best friends.

The Oyaks took my mother and kept her hidden in their apartment. Mrs. Oyak occasionally went to see my dad at his place of work. On one of those visits, he told her he had heard that all the Jewish people working in that place would be taken away and shot. Upon hearing this, Mrs. Oyak said, "Come home with me."

All of the Sczygiel family have passed away except for one of the daughters, Joanna, who has a daughter named Grazyna, whose own daughter lives in New York. Grazyna and her husband come from Poland every year to visit the daughter, and we all get together.

Not quite a year ago, I received a call from Grazyna. She said that she had something very special to tell me. We got together the following day. This is what she said. She never had before, to me or my parents.

Mrs. Sczygiel had shopped quite often at Sarotina, my parents' business. She hadn't been able to afford to buy the more expensive, hand-dipped chocolates, yet, coming home and opening her package, she had always found expensive pieces that my parents knew the girls liked.

When she ran into my father on that fateful day outside of the ghetto, the memory of my mother and father's kindness came to her mind. The remembrance made her go up to my father and offer to try and save my life, even though she knew that, if I was found in their home, the whole family would be killed by the Nazis.

And because of that remembrance my parents and I survived the Holocaust.

Bio Note

Ruth Gruener came to America in January 1949. Since her parents didn't have an apartment, she lived with her uncle and aunt for eight months while attending high school. She attended Brooklyn College though, marrying young and having a baby, wasn't able to finish her studies.

When her children got older, she studied interior design and worked with her husband in their interior design firm. When he retired, she took a real estate course and sold houses. Between other activities, she also gave piano and accordion lessons.

Loving to play with children, she became a clown as well and worked as a clown for almost two years.

For the past 15 years she has volunteered at the Museum of Jewish Heritage in Manhattan, where she gives tours and speaks to groups about her life during the Holocaust. She has spoken in schools in Arizona, Alabama, Pennsylvania, Connecticut, New Jersey, and all boroughs of New York and is the author of *Destined to Live*, a Holocaust memoir.

GROWING UP IN THE HOLOCAUST DAYS

Zahava Szàsz Stessel

THE HOLOCAUST IN HUNGARY didn't begin with the deportation. There were the preceding waves of anti-Jewish laws that made life for Jewish residents hard and challenging.

In my family, my grandparents owned two meat stores. One, for kosher meat, was located in the synagogue courtyard; the other, which sold non-kosher products, was on the main street. The banning of ritual slaughter was among the first anti-Jewish laws enacted in 1938. While some merchants resorted to trading in swine meat, my grandfather, a religious person, opted to sell poultry, whose kosher killing was still permitted. The job, however, involved hard work for my mother and grandmother, and it wasn't too profitable.

A variety of economic restrictions also embittered the lives of Jewish merchants like my father. One of them governed the allocation of leather goods from the limited supply available. While non-Jewish merchants could carry such goods, my father could not sell any leather products, including basic necessities like shoes, in the family's retail clothing store.

Despite the growing economic adversity, my family still maintained the impression of a prosperous family unit, as before. An observant teenager, I recognized my parents' stressful and precarious situation. In my spare time, after school, I began to look for work, such as the spinning of Angora rabbit fur for thread, a vocation and trade created by Jews who faced the closing of other sources of income. I saved the money I earned, which wasn't very much, as security for when my parents would need it.

At the public school I attended, students who could afford it continued after four years in a private middle school. Seeing my parents' economic distress, I announced that I wanted to stay in the public school.

The following year, my sister registered for the private middle school. I felt a bit uncomfortable when people commented that I didn't really care for study and wasn't very serious about school. Yet I was pleased that, by saving my tuition, my parents had been able to allow my sister to attend.

Eventually, the Jewish students attending public school were segregated from the other students.

We were in a separate classroom, where Grades 1–8 were combined, and not much professional teaching occurred. My sister attended the private school until April 1944, when we were all taken to the nearby ghetto of Kosice and then to Auschwitz.

Since my sister and I, two teenagers, were close in age, and believing that we were twins, Dr. Josef Mengele directed us to the side of the living when we got off the train. Mengele needed twins for his experiments. We cried and tried to protest, as my mother and grandmother, walking arm in arm, were forced to continue on that road of no return—my mother looking back with those painful, puzzling eyes, and my little grandmother's desperate, loving expression have accompanied me since on all the thoroughfares of my life.

When we said that we were not twins, we were allowed to stay with all the others who were selected for work. We endured these selections with the constant fear that the SS would separate us.

At the end of September 1944, we were transferred to Bergen-Belsen. Before leaving, we received half of a small loaf of bread and a bit of salami for the road. It was the first time in months that we felt a bit of excitement. We didn't even know how lucky we were to leave Auschwitz alive. Unable to accept the cruelest reality, we hoped that they had taken our parents somewhere else as well.

On the way to Bergen-Belsen, the German guard watching us allowed the heavy sliding door of the freight car to be kept open, and we could observe the changing scenery. During daylight, as the train passed through agricultural land, we could see cows and workers doing their jobs. We stared, not believing that the earth had continued on its regular orbit and the world had sustained its normalcy while we were in that other world in Auschwitz.

At night, the train passed towns and cities with lighted windows. We thought of the people behind the lights—that they were free and lived their usual lives. Only we were the outcasts, our world destroyed.

At Bergen-Belsen, registrars filled out cards with our personal data. Many things about that place have been erased from my mind, but the registration at the tables that stood outside the tents I remember very clearly. Maybe it impressed me that people wanted to know about us. They asked our names, ages, parents' names, and places of birth. Then my sister, Erzsike, received the number 5419 and I became number 5420.

Going to the latrine one day, I heard a familiar voice calling me from the other end. Pulling Erzsike with me and following the sound, we reached Marta Krausz, my best friend and classmate. Marta was full of life at home, and that made me so happy to be her friend. We had lived close by, shared our teenage secrets, and, having no telephones, visited each other at all hours of the day.

From the ghetto, we had been taken in different transports to Auschwitz and lost contact with one another. By the time we met in Bergen-Belsen, Marta was disheveled; Erzsike described her later as sickly looking, but I didn't see it. I looked at her brown eyes, still expressing the childhood faith and optimism that I liked so much about her. Marta and her sister, Vera, two years her senior, had arrived in Bergen-Belsen later than we did, after working in a factory and surviving a death march. They had also been separated from their mother and grandmother.

We hugged each other, and tears began to cloud our eyes when Marta's group had to leave. Deeply affected by the meeting, I was thinking how seeing Marta gave me both pain and some happy feelings of reconnection to that old world that was so far away from us. How nice it would be, I thought, if the four of us could be together. We would almost have the five-person line the SS required completed in *Appel*. As we were not allowed to walk around in the camp, I started to visit the latrine every time I could, taking Erzsike with me. We stayed in the latrine as long as it was possible, but I never met Marta. One of those days, as I was again in line with Erzsike for the latrine in search of her, we were told that there would be an *Appel* for selection to work.

We were all excited, but I still insisted on going to the latrine, hoping that maybe Marta would be there. Erzsike was worried, but she came with me, only to be disappointed again. We hurried back and started to get ready for the *Appel*.

That was at the beginning of December. My friend Isabella quickly gave me a comb she had borrowed, and both Erzsike and I combed our hair. Margit, Isabella's sister, admired my blond hair, which looked good since growing out a bit. Margit's compliments gave me some confidence. We stood in line to wash our hands and faces from water in the pipe outside. We were told that we would not have to undress for the selection. Erzsike, who was more resourceful than I, obtained a piece of cloth for me to put on as a belt for my dress, which was far too wide on me. This way it looked better. We smoothed out our dresses and prayed that they would not separate us. As we stood on *Appel* in the muddy field, the selection process began. Our hearts hardened with fear as we passed the committee. To our luck and advantage, there was a shortage of prisoners and slave workers, so the SS was more lenient in selection. They passed the two of us. We blessed our fortune; and even today, as I am writing these lines, I am grateful to God that we were assigned to the fourth and the last transport to Markkleeberg, a work camp near Leipzig.

I had no way to let Marta know about my departure. With all the fear and excitement of leaving, I still thought of Marta's loving face. How long did she continue looking and hoping to find me? Would she realize, knowing the unpredictably of camp life, that it was not my fault? Thinking of our magical games and childhood play, I was sending her my mental note of love and friendship forever. Trusting that Marta had received my message on its miraculous wings of childhood magic, I felt a bit better.

Had I known then Marta's tragic fate, and that I would never see her again, my pain would have been even stronger. Suffering from typhus, Vera died a day before liberation, and Marta survived only a few days longer.

Of all the events in the camp, the memory of meeting Marta is one that never fades. When I see those terrible photographs of skeletons awaiting burial from Bergen-Belsen, I see my friend Marta's sad face among them.

My sister and I had survived, in addition to Auschwitz and Bergen-Belsen, a slave labor camp in Markkleeberg, Germany, where we worked for a factory producing airplane parts, even though we could hardly reach the machine. Toward the end of the war we were led to a forced death march but were liberated by the Russian army.

In 1945, we returned to our looted home in Abaujszanto, which was occupied by strangers. We had lost our parents, grandparents, friends, and schoolmates in Auschwitz. .

Our uncle Joseph Reinitz, and his wife, Rozi, contacted us from Budapest. They had no children and had survived the war. Wanting to help, they suggested we move in with them and attend high school. Broken in soul and spirit, however, we were unable to sit down, study, and resume our previous lives. Eventually we joined a Zionist group of young people to start a new life in Palestine. We said a painful goodbye to our aunt and uncle, whom we would never see again.

Our voyage took us on a long journey that ended in another forced confinement, this time under the British in Cyprus.

After we reached Kibbutz Heftzibah, in 1947, we settled down to everyday life. I began to realize that getting an education was very important for me. My sister and I requested a transfer from the kibbutz to the agricultural school of Ajanot, which had been opened to orphans such as ourselves. After graduation, we settled in Haifa.

There, the study that I wouldn't have been allowed to pursue during the Holocaust years became my first priority. I found a job as a caretaker for a six-year-old boy stricken with polio. In the evening, I attended remedial classes towards a high school diploma. Before I could complete it, I met my husband, and fate led us to the United States.

In New York, I continued my mission to get a high

school diploma. I attended classes at night while my husband babysat for our two young daughters. My sister, who had remained in Israel, had also continued her education, and became a registered nurse. She eventually was in charge of the emergency trauma unit of the Rambam Hospital in Haifa.

As for me, I went on to complete a bachelor of arts and a masters degree. While employed as a librarian at the New York Public Library on Fifth Avenue, I began taking classes at New York University, for my doctorate. Eventually, close to the age of sixty, I earned a Ph.D. The theme of my work, which was subsequently published, is the history of my town before and during the Holocaust. I have continued expanding my boundaries by writing another book, as my childhood Holocaust trauma is still leading my way.

Bio Note

Zahava Szàsz Stessel, Ph.D., is the author of *Wine and Thorns in Tokay Valley, Jewish Life in Hungary: The History of Abaújszántó* (1995) and *Snow Flowers: Hungarian Jewish Women in an Airplane Factory, Markkleeberg, Germany* (2009).

DEAREST MAMA

Rina Nudel

Dearest Mama, I have already lived thirty-one years more than you.

I never had a chance to send you the flowers or the beautiful card that you so richly deserved. I do not remember your face. There are no pictures of you. All lost. But I have a vague outline of your being. I remember the warmth and love. I was *"dus kind,"* the baby, the youngest of five. I remember your calling me your crown (*"dem king"*), for the baby. You were the symbol of love and goodness. But all of a sudden, you were plucked away from me, and all of us children.

It is August 1942. I am ten years old.

The memory is vivid, painful, and tear-provoking, sometimes out of nowhere. Nazis surround our street. We hear shouts, screams: *"Raus, raus!"* They go from apartment to apartment. I am petrified and ask Mama what will be, what will happen to us. To me, she seems calm and composed. She is standing in the kitchen, next to a big metal basin filled with laundry. She tells me not to worry, *"Mein kind."* She will explain to the Nazis. She spoke perfect German. The family needs her.

But that will not be the case. Pleading and begging will not help.

All of a sudden, the shouting stops for a few moments. We hope we are spared.

But then the dreaded loud knock on the door. They almost skipped our apartment, only to be reminded by the Ukrainian soldier that there is one more place in the back. The horrifying loud knock. A Nazi soldier with a helmet, rifle, and bayonet enters the apartment, screaming, *"Raus, raus."* Mama has no chance to explain or say a word. She is struck with the rifle butt. We are mortified. It felt like death had come upon us. All of a sudden, Hesio, my older brother, appears. I've never found out how he knew we were in trouble. I am so happy to see him. His face is tear-stained. He tries to bribe the Nazi with his watch, a bottle of whiskey—but nothing helps. He is chased and beaten with the bottle.

I feel paralyzed, too shocked to cry, and all I hear is Hesio crying, knowing that he is losing his mother and little sister. "Mama, Mama, Rennusia," he whispers. He hands us a big loaf of round black bread. The picture of his crying face is etched forever in my memory.

Mother and I are walking to the street. Mother loses her shoe. Shouts, screams, and crying are mingled in one horrifying sound.

I hold on to her in horror, asking constantly, "What will happen to us? What will happen to us? What will Lonek, Misko, and Dana say when they come home and we are not there?"

Mama does not cry. She hugs me close to her. We are taken to the city jail, and from there to Janowska Lager, and after that my memory is all scrambled: barbed wire, a lot of fences, a lot of people shuffled from place to place. At night, huge reflectors make sure people will not escape. Piles of luggage, containers of jewelry, eye glasses, money, from everywhere; rail tracks are visible, and cargo wagons to transfer people to killing camps. Later on, we find out that, from

Lwow, they were taken to Belzec, a notoriously cruel camp that had maybe ten survivors.

Mother is holding my hand tight trying to cross to another group, thinking they will be released, but we were chased by an SS soldier back to where we came from. Our food is the loaf of bread my brother gave us. I do not remember getting anything else, maybe some water. This nightmare lasts three or four days.

ON THE LAST MORNING, mother is very quiet. It is a sunny, warm day. She hugs me very tight and points to a small group of people down the road. She tells me, "Renusia, these people will be released." She must have realized that she would never make it. She wants desperately to save me. She pushes me away from her toward that small group, and says, "Run, run!" I cry, but when I turn around, she is gone. Not knowing what to do, I cross to that small group. I approach them. The people are frightened and don't want me around. They are scared I could jeopardize their release. They push me, but I have no place to go. A short Nazi soldier is checking the documents of that selected group, to make sure they can be released. He does not see me. A Ukrainian soldier from a high watch tower is screaming to the Nazi, "The little girl is running away!" But the Nazi does not hear him and does not understand Ukrainian.

This is how I escape the gates of Hell.

OUTSIDE THE GATES OF JANOWSKA LAGER, my brothers are waiting. They have come there every day, hoping they can get us out.

When they see me, they hug me and ask, "Where is Mama?"

All I can say is, "I don't know." I am numb and disheveled. I do not cry. My thin braids are muddled. I am still wearing my green summer coat.

The crying began days later.

We never saw you, Mama, again. You gave birth to me twice. I remember your soul, Mama. Your goodness has stayed with me, my children, and my grandchildren whom you would be so proud of.

Bio Note

Rina Nudel was born in Poland in 1932, the youngest of five children. She was taken with her mother to the Janowska concentration camp, where her mother saved her. After being hidden in Christian homes, she fled to the Ukraine with her two brothers and her sister, using forged papers. She reached Palestine in 1944, where she graduated from Rambam Hospital as a registered nurse and became a nursing instructor. When she retired from nursing, she became a gallery educator at the Museum of Jewish Heritage.

Rina came to the United States in 1957 with her husband and eighteen-month-old baby. She is proud of a successful forty-year nursing career, and even more proud of her married son and daughter, and eight grandchildren.

A WEB OF TRAGEDIES

Helga Shepard

IT STARTED WHEN I WAS SIX and my parents told me I would be going for a ride on a train with my older brother, Martin. He was fifteen, nine years older than I was. How exciting! I worshiped Martin—it would be an adventure!

They did not say that the journey would take us far away from Berlin, through Germany, and that I was leaving family and love and all that I had known behind. Martin and I were leaving on the Kindertransport for England in May 1939. It must have fallen to Martin to tell me of the rise of warfare against the Jews, and that our parents were sending us to safety.

On arrival in London, we found out that mandatory education in England extended only until the age of fourteen. So at fifteen he was sent to a farm to work, and I went on to Nottingham, to a relative of my father named Esta Green.

In September 1939, Hitler unleashed a ferocious attack on Poland, and war was declared by Great Britain. My father, Jakob, was at once arrested and sent to Sachsenhausen concentration camp. My mother, Kayla, had a visa for Great Britain as a cook, but gave up her chance at freedom in order to obtain Jakob's release. And that is what she miraculously did, for she was resourceful and found out that one country, China, would accept refugees without a visa and so procured his release from Sachsenhausen on condition of leaving Germany within a week. She had bought him a steamship ticket to Shanghai, and they went to Italy.

In August 1940, Jakob boarded the S.S. *Conte Verde* for Shanghai, but he sailed alone, leaving my mother behind, without papers or money, in wartime Italy. They had sent all their money to his relative in England to take care of their children, and there was no money for her passage.

My mother was soon arrested as a refugee and, on

her release, smuggled herself to France, to Marseilles, hoping to find a ship that would take her to safety. There again, she was imprisoned for being a refugee. On her release after ten weeks, a French policeman told her to be wary, for the Gestapo was assiduously intent on finding Jews who were trying to escape from war-torn France. For a while she managed to keep body and soul together, but the occupying Nazis watched the ports, and the railroad stations, and it was at a bus stop that she was arrested again.

That happened in 1942, and she was sent to Camp de Gurs, in the south of France, on the border with Spain.

It was a place of misery and starvation, for in winter the rains came, which turned the ground to mud, and the rats came out. Every other night, names were called, and people were put on trains taking them east to the concentration camps. My mother's name was called, and she was put on a train. But four people jumped off, and then she did, too.

But the train was traveling fast, and she was knocked unconscious. When she recovered her senses, she found herself back in Camp de Gurs with her clothes all bloody and a bandage around her head. She gave up on her life. She had wanted to see her children one more time. But the war defeated her; she saw no way out. She wanted to end her suffering.

She climbed to the top of a water tower with the intention of jumping off, but a guard who had spotted her ran over and grabbed her.

She was taken below and locked up in a room for fourteen days. The French doctor in camp arranged to send my mother to a psychiatric hospital nearby in Pau. She remained there for the rest of the war and beyond, desperately depressed.

When I arrived in Nottingham, I found Esta Green was married to David. They had a daughter, Sara, and a son, Henry, and lived in a large house with a maid, Kathleen, who slept upstairs. I was sent to school, where I soon learned the language and to my delight, also learned to read. After a few months I was sent to London: I dare say they wearied of me. My mother's brother Uncle Herman and his wife, Margarita, collected me from Bloomsbury House, which had sent a notice saying there was a package for them, so I was told. It was in 1940 and Hitler had launched aerial attacks against England, first in the south against the small British air force, then nightly against London, raining bombs and bringing destroyed houses, raging fires, and death. But the British spirit did not break, with the Prime Minister Winston Churchill's defiant "We shall never surrender!"

However, my aunt and uncle decided to evacuate to Oxford and took me with them. My aunt found a Catholic school for me, which I enjoyed. They decided to return to London and left me with a lady, Miss Emily Horne, who had a private school, and another boarder besides me. Miss Horne was tall and good natured. She had a cheerful routine, and I felt safe and comfortable with her. Upstairs was the school room with shelves along three walls filled with books. I read *Lorna Doone* there and discovered a wild Scottish world.

Miss Horne made me flannel petticoats with bright flowers embroidered just above the hem.

One day I found myself back in Nottingham, in the garden in back of the large house. I was eight years old and felt small, surrounded by giants. A question came down to me: 'Don't you want to come back here to live?' I was horrified, leave the warmth of Miss Horne's house? I hated the thought of that, but I was much too frightened to say so. I was terrified, trying to grapple with a situation way beyond my eight-year-old's ability to handle. I managed to mutter, "Let me have a run around the garden," but the courage to follow my instincts and refuse did not appear. I hung my head and gave in. It was a trap, I realized, for the household had changed drastically.

It was wartime and the cooks, gardeners, and chauffeurs had all joined the armed forces to fight the enemy. Kathleen the maid had left to work in a factory and Esta Green plotted to turn me into the maid. It was my lot to clean and sweep and dust, to mow the lawn and wash the greasy dishes after supper and make tea and toast for their breakfast and put it on a tray and bring it upstairs to their bedroom door before dashing off to school. But nothing I did pleased her.

She said, "If there is a right way to do things Helga will find the wrong way." The atmosphere was strained, ominous. I was caught in a venomous situation—anything I did was bad. The labels of stupid, clumsy, and fool were welded to me. She began to hit me and why was there a horse whip hanging on the wall in the kitchen? The lashes felt like fire and raised purple welts. She let her son whip me too and he drew blood. Sadly, I believed her for I had no one to talk to. I thought I had a bad character and as my inner landscape changed, I built a wall around me not to attract attention, not to offend.

One day in the kitchen there was a toast rack

where opened letters were kept.

I recognized the long, narrow envelope as being one that had messages from my father, through the International Red Cross. The envelope had been opened and I drew out the sheet. I had not seen it before. It said, *Mr. Uszerowicz has not yet learned of his son's death*. I had to reread it to understand that my brother had died, for I had been told he had gone into the Royal Air Force. My world shattered. Now I was all alone. No one noticed my despair, nor that I was in tears most of the time. My parents were long gone; now I was like an orphan and all alone.

Several years later, I was sent to Rusthall, a hostel with other refugee children.

At the end of the war, in 1945, I was sent to a boarding school, Bunce Court, in Kent. In London briefly, with my aunt and uncle, I found out how death had struck my brother. He had gone to a swimming pool with a friend. In the water Martin suddenly got cramps and found himself in deep water, unable to swim.

He was thrashing around. His friend swam over. Martin was frightened and clung to him so frantically that the boy panicked and tore off Martin's hands and so Martin drowned. So here was tragedy and death.

No use asking why no one noticed or helped. He stays with me in a fantasy relationship—I ask him questions and talk to him.

It was at the beginning of 1947 that my father returned from China to Europe.

Through the International Red Cross, he knew where my mother was and found her in hospital, in Pau, in southern France She was deeply depressed. He decided there would be more help in Paris and took her there. It was planned that I would join them in September, later in the year.

Eight years after our separation, three survivors of our shattered family were to reunite. I was sent away when I was six and now I had just turned fifteen. My brother was dead. My Orthodox father, Jakob, had a bitter situation to deal with. How to support the three of us in a country that was foreign to him, whose language he did not speak, mourning the loss of his son? The feelings about his son's death were unbearably painful and impossible to banish. It is against nature for the young to die before the old.

PARIS READ THE SIGNS as the train pulled into the station. People were reaching for their luggage and then getting off the train, greeting family and friends, and there were hugs and laughter and chatter. They picked up their bags and began to drift off. Slowly the platform emptied and still I waited.

I began to realize that something had gone wrong for no one came to claim me.

I could not turn around and go back to London. That was finished and over.

My parents and I had been writing to each other and I had an envelope in my pocket with their address. I walked through the station and found a taxi.

Somehow I had some French money and I gave the driver their address.

It was a tiny hotel in the Marais section. I got out and spoke to the manager. He said my parents had gone to get me and I should wait for them to return.

I waited and suddenly a tall, stout woman surged into the room and cried out, "'I saw you! I saw you at the station! I sent away a princess! You looked like an English schoolgirl!" She had sent away a pampered six-year-old, and, eight years later, I was obviously a huge disappointment. I said there had been a war and I had been sent to many different places.

My father boiled with strong feelings. Within a week, enraged at me, he told me to go back to England. My mother jumped between us when he raised a chair to smash over my head.

I sometimes think of commissioning an artist to show how we were at our reunion: three marble columns each grievously hurt in its own way…but the real tragedy is their inability to communicate with each other. There was little talk and no listening. My brother's death brought unbearable pain and grief.

With my three languages I found work at 16. In 1953 the family came to America. My father opened a store, I found work and went to school at night for sixteen years, found a profession and work.

Now I feel enormous gratitude in my life for I have three children and enjoy life immensely.

Bio Note

Helga Shepard started her education in England from age six to fourteen. She resumed her education in the U.S. in 1955 for sixteen years. In 1981 she received her Masters of Science in Social Work. She worked in the Board of Education as a Bilingual Social Worker. Now, she is a Docent at the Holocaust Memorial and Tolerance Center of Nassau County. She married Albert Shepard in 1957; they have three children: Glenn, Suzanne, and Lenore. She has three grandchildren.

FIGHTING THE NAZI WAR MACHINE

Essie Schor

AT THE TIME OF THE INVASION, the Germans and Russians split Poland into two. The Germans took the West, and the Russians the East, where my town was located. Later the Germans would break the treaty and invade our part of Poland, too. Late one afternoon in July 1941, we heard the sound of bombs. Neighbors up and down the street ran out of their houses crying, "War!" The war had come to us.

When the bombing stopped, it was eerily silent. We were grateful that our house had not been hit, but we were frightened and panicked to see what would happen next. We did not have to wait long to hear that the Nazis had invaded and ordered the Jews to bring everything they owned to the town square. My parents parted with silverware, candlesticks, and all their possessions, as had all the other Jews in town. Our lives were completely changed. At first we were in a state of shock. Along with other Jewish children, I was not allowed to return to my old school and learned how to stay alive from day to day. Food was hard to come by. My family used whatever money we had to buy food from nearby farmers, and we children went scouting for wood so we could cook and keep warm by the stove.

Before the ghetto was completed, my parents knew that we had a better chance to survive outside of town. We were able to borrow a wagon and travel to the outskirts of Novogrudek, where our relatives, the Bielskis, lived. The family owned a large farmstead, far from the center, and allowed us to sleep in the barn that their sons guarded with scythes. The Bielskis were physically strong and well educated, and being in the countryside knew how to defend themselves. But having another large Jewish family to continue living in the barn indefinitely was impossible and dangerous, and not knowing where else to hide, we returned to our old home.

I was just sixteen when the Nazis came to Novogrudek (a part of Poland, now in Belarus), and began their first pogrom (*aktzia* in Polish) against the Jewish people. On that summer day, four thousand Jews were killed, including my mother and all my brothers. My father and I, and seven hundred other Jews, were left alive and herded into prison-like conditions in the ghetto they established. These seven hundred created a labor force for the Germans, sewing and mending uniforms, fixing machinery and vehicles, laying bricks, and building roads. I was given a work permit, and each morning I was counted by the police and marched out with other Jewish workers to build an ammunition storage facility. When work was finished, we were forced to line up, counted again, and marched back to the ghetto. After the murder of my family, I was always disoriented and in shock, but I was given a work permit and marched with my father to work sites. Somehow, the German work permit became an official document for me, and the routine of hard physical work provided a strange sense of distraction and security from the chaos and murders we witnessed.

While we were living in the ghetto, a Christian farmer friend supplied us with vegetables, milk, and bread, which he delivered to the ghetto fence in exchange for my family's valuables, which we still were hiding. The man also shared news from the outside world and told us that a group of Russian fighters, called "partisans," had banded together to fight the Nazis in the wild forests of the area (*pushcha*). Initially, the Partisans were prisoners of war who had escaped from the Nazis and were fighting their former captors, but I soon learned that the group included, not only Russian partisans, but also Jewish soldiers and civilians, many trained in the Polish army. I was excited and hopeful when I discovered that my cousins, the Bielski brothers, were leaders of such a partisan group, and I never stopped thinking about where and how to run away from the ghetto and join my relatives in the forest. I planned ways of escape and often spoke with my father about it, but he was afraid to leave.

It was not easy to be accepted into the group. At first, they called only on young men who had served in the Polish army and knew how to fight, but later they accepted as many Jews as possible and spread their net wider. Later the Jewish people built a tunnel, and some two hundred people who had not been killed escaped through the tunnel to join the Partisans.

Confident that my Bielski cousins liked me and

would accept me into the Partisans, my father understood that I had a better chance of survival outside of the Ghetto, and that I was young and healthy and should flee.

Cautiously, shaking but silent, I left the ghetto at night. I feared that I would be killed on the spot but fortunately was able to hide from the patrolling police. I escaped by squeezing through a hole in the ghetto fence and headed for the home of one of my friendly Polish teachers for help. Shocked to see me so upset, she fed me, changed my clothes, got rid of my jacket with the Jewish star, and declared that, with my blond hair and new clothes, I no longer resembled a Jew. Still, I could not sleep in her house, because if the police came around, she would be killed along with my father, who was still living in the ghetto. Safer to spend the night hiding in the cornfields among the tall, high ripe corn.

That night was the longest night of my life. I managed to remain in the field all night. Thirsty and hungry, feet bleeding, I had to keep listening for the police, and I tried to calm myself by praying constantly and not be overwhelmed by terror and despair. It was a nightmarish game of hide-and-seek that could end in death. I prayed that I could run away from death, and find my cousins, the Partisans. The small group lived in the woods but sent trusted peasants to convince other Jews to follow.

Word had gotten to the Bielskis that I was hiding in the cornfields. In a clearing, I saw a man, a friend of theirs, waiting for me, casually leaning against a tree. I remember walking with him fifteen kilometers that night along a narrow, winding country road, partly hidden by trees, arriving hours later at an isolated house at the edge of the woods. He led me from a peasant's house, into the forest. Branches slapped in my face and caught my clothes, and my wounded feet were constantly in pain, but I didn't complain. In fact, I couldn't utter a word. With every step, I began to feel free and hopeful in my heart that I was about to become one of the first twenty-five Jews to join my cousins, the Bielski Brothers, in an encampment that would eventually save twelve hundred Jews!

At last, I walked into a clearing deep in the woods. As I peered into the dissolving morning mist, I discerned people sitting around an open fire, shielded by trees. They were singing hopeful songs of freedom in low voices. I can recall the sound of a murmuring brook mingling with a melody and harmonizing with their song.

Three blurry figures stepped out of the fog, and I recognized them as my cousins, Tuvia, Asael, and Zus. We hugged and kissed each other, and I quietly cried. Wrapped tightly in their arms, I felt safe for the first time since German bombs fell on our town, and I drifted off to sleep in a bed of leaves in the forest.

Learning to Be a Partisan

We often joined forces with the Russian Partisan group because we depended on the same food resource from farmers, and used Russian ammunition. "A bullet from a rifle in Jewish hands kills just the same as a rifle in Russian hands," Tuvia said as I trained to use one. Living in the forest, I no longer felt like cattle, herded into the ghetto.

Our group had to move constantly. German soldiers were looking for us everywhere, and sometimes villagers living nearby would inform. Once, we had to leave in a hurry when the Nazis discovered the hoofprints of our cows in the snow. This was a different kind of fear. We had changed from being caged animals to armed warriors who could defend themselves.

Another relative, a machinist by trade, fixed all our guns and collected ammunition. A handy and resourceful older man, he fashioned a rifle and later a gun out of broken parts for me. Holding the weapon for the first time, I panicked, but still slung the weapon over my shoulder. I was learning how to shoot, and soon the lessons became part of me. After those instructions, I found, in the beginning, that I was the only female in the group. I was trained and taught, step by step by a friendly Polish army soldier, how to clean, service, and maintain a weapon, how to load and take aim, fire, and reload. Within a week, I had learned everything about the weapon and felt comfortable. My gun and my cousins became my family and protectors when I became part of the military patrol.

I was happy with my new, challenging, and dangerous life. I learned the sounds of the forest, about pine and fir, birch and spruce trees, and how to recognize the songs of various birds. I also helped with the cooking, went on missions to acquire strategic information, and obtained supplies. Remembering my life in the forests, I feel I was reborn only seventy- five years ago!

In 1944, the Russians were on the offensive, on the road to Berlin. The Germans were in retreat and were trying to kill as many of us as possible. At one point, the Russian and German armies crossed paths, and we were caught in the crossfire. The German soldiers continued the attack, and many men from the Bielski partisan camp were killed and still more lost their lives during the course of our struggle. I am very proud to have been a guerrilla fighter in the resistance to the Nazi war machine. Spying and watching for German soldiers, equipped with a rifle and participating in missions to uncover strategic information and find supplies imparted a wonderful sense of self-esteem to a sixteen-year-old girl-soldier, which I still treasure today!

Bio Note

Essie Schor, a former schoolteacher who worked in New York City, is one of the last surviving Bielski Partisans. After retiring, she published her book, *Essie: The True Story of a Teenage Fighter in the Bielski Partisans*. The film *Defiance* includes a part of her story. She lives in New York City.

She was married to Jerry Schor and has a daughter and grandchildren who live in Philadelphia.

www.ingramcontent.com/pod-product-compliance
Lightning Source LLC
Chambersburg PA
CBHW020904090426
42736CB00008B/488